'Philip Stevens has produced an engrossing and engaging account of adult higher learning in Britain, which testifies to its power to change lives. His book is at once a survey of the variety available and evidence of the continuing importance of these opportunities both for individuals and for UK society as a whole.'

Lesley Smith, Professor of Medieval Intellectual History, Harris Manchester College, University of Oxford

'Philip Stevens draws extensively on the accounts of individual students to show that anyone, of any age, can benefit today from a movement that continues to build on the pioneering work of early "benefactors". There is no better way to illustrate the value of taking the first, sometimes giant, step to adult learning than by telling the stories of learners such as those featured in his book.'

Suzanna Jackson, Warden, Mary Ward Settlement

Rita and Gerald

This book is dedicated to the memories of Jack Stevens and Malcolm Williams

Rita and Gerald

Adult learning in Britain today

Philip Stevens

A Trentham Book
Institute of Education Press

First published in 2015 by the Institute of Education Press, University of London, 20 Bedford Way, London WC1H 0AL

ioepress.co.uk

British Library Cataloguing in Publication Data:
A catalogue record for this publication is available from the British Library

ISBNs
978-1-85856-624-5 (paperback)
978-1-85856-637-5 (PDF eBook)
978-1-85856-638-2 (ePub eBook)
978-1-85856-639-9 (Kindle eBook)

Typeset by Quadrant Infotech (India) Pvt Ltd
Printed by CPI Group (UK) Ltd, Croydon, CR0 4YY

Contents

List of figures

Acknowledgements

I am indebted to Gillian Klein of Trentham Books at IOE Press. Without her support and encouragement this book would not have seen the light of day. If Gillian helped to get this book into shape, any errors of fact or judgement remain my own.

The book could not have been written without the support of Christine Perry, Bryony Merrit, and Caroline McDonald at Birkbeck College; Imogen Petit, Maddy Fisk, Tasneem Khan, and Suzanna Jackson at the Mary Ward Centre; Satnam Gill and Gillian Welch at the Working Men's College; Wendy Burrell at the Open University Student Association; Professor Audrey Mullender, former Principal of Ruskin College; and Professor Lesley Smith at Harris Manchester College, Oxford.

Special thanks are due to an old friend and fellow traveller, Professor Fred Inglis, for agreeing to write the Preface.

And last but not least, enormous thanks to the men and women who told me their experiences, memories and stories. From Harris Manchester College, Oxford: Revd Andrew Brown, Angie Johnson, and Sandra Valdini; from the Working Men's College: Tracy Elba-Porter, Dilwara Taluker, Hazel Stephenson, Wilfredo Garcia-Sarria, and Rosh Keegan; from Birkbeck College: Mustapha Sow, Bridget Fuller, and Gerald Nathanson; from the Mary Ward Centre: Annalisa Cacorgiani and Shanti Claire; from Ruskin College: Steve Barrett, Bill Haywood, Adrian Pritchard, David Tanguay, Rowan Padmore, Adrienne Lowing and Frances Cage; and from the Open University: Lucia Gomez-Santana, Claire Baker, Simon Binns, Julie Cobbin, Louise Clark, Bill Brown, Alex Farr, Sally Black, Rose Papai, Dr Catherine Lee, and Allen Jack.

About the author

Philip Stevens served as a firefighter in the London Fire Brigade in his early 20s, before A levels at evening classes secured him a place at university. A BA Hons from Liverpool University, a PGCE from Worcester College of HE, and an MA and PhD in Philosophy of Education from the Institute of Education, University of London, followed within a few years.

Following his conversion from firefighter to academic, he taught in schools, colleges, and universities for over 25 years, first in both special and mainstream schools in London during the 1980s. In 1990 he was appointed Head of Adult and Community Learning at a community college in Plymouth. In addition to his full-time post, he taught philosophy of art for the Open University for 12 years as an associate lecturer.

Philip Stevens's main academic interest lies in aesthetics and in the 1990s he was awarded visiting fellowships at the University of Tennessee, the Institute of Education (University of London), and Merton College, Oxford, where he explored the role of arts education in the United States and Israel. His love of art began in the basement of a house in Woburn Square, then home to the philosophy of education department of the Institute of Education. It was in the dingy Bloomsbury basement that he and the rest of his class listened in awe to the wonderful philosophy tutor Ray Elliot. It is this ability to inspire that has driven his career in education.

Following early retirement in 2008, Philip Stevens turned to writing, publishing three books on the social history of sport in London. His critically acclaimed biography of the late football manager John Lyall was published in 2014.

A former secretary of a local branch of the Workers' Educational Association and chair of the South West Open College Network, Dr Stevens is passionate about adult learning and the life-changing opportunities it offers mature students. Concerned about the threats to the sector from successive governments, he began researching and writing about the history of adult education, compiling an impressive archive of the experiences of more than 150 adult learners from six of the major adult education institutions in the UK. The result of the research is this book, a robust defence of adult learning in modern Britain and a study of its power to transform lives and achieve social change.

Preface

The vast, unwarlike imperium of adult education has been fortunate in its historians. To this impressive legion, Phil Stevens is the latest and wholly congenial addition. He retells the stories of several of the heroes and heroines of this strange, expansive institution, which, I would claim, is one of the most impressive achievements not only of national education but also of the nation's democracy. It is worth pausing over the mention he makes of one enemy of democracy, Margaret Thatcher, who during her office as Secretary of State for Education greeted a senior officer of adult education by jeering at what she believed to be a curriculum contrived for 'housewives' hobbies'.

The lie is given to this crass remark by a woman who turned out to be not only a commendable novelist in the great field of Victorian fiction, Mrs Humphrey Ward, but who as Mary Ward was pioneer and architect of our titular institution, a moral fable brought out with admirable force in the present book. Every intellectual achievement must be maintained and remade by the ceremonies of ancestor worship. Phil Stevens gives Mary Ward and John Ruskin pride of place in the nineteenth century, and then proceeds by way of such great names as R.H. Tawney and a conversational medley among which Messrs Fieldhouse, Harrison, and Shaw are honoured by well-deserved eulogy, all crowned by the now-legendary writings and teachings of Raymond Williams, E.P. Thompson, and Richard Hoggart.

This latter trinity is crucial to our understanding of both the political and pedagogic significance of Phil Stevens's subject. Each of these figures came to understand and make explicit the principles that order the structures of knowledge and, intrinsic to those structures, the selection and interpretation of the human experience out of which that knowledge is formed. Only in those ordinary, commonplace, and domestic settings of primary school classrooms, working men's institutes, church halls, and the echoing upstairs rooms of local pubs could the knot have been tied between individual sensibilities and the formal arrangements of official learning and scholarship. The supreme achievement of adult education was to insist on the necessity of that encounter. Both science and literature – the very substance of culture – are effortfully contrived out of the collision between the moral imagination of society and the demands of life itself.

This gentle-mannered, scrupulous, and accessible book works in this honoured tradition, never more so than when it heeds the words of the author's own students and those of other students he has invited to have their say. He laments the recent passing of a sharp political conscience from the domain of adult education, and one must mourn in his company. Nonetheless, for myself, I wonder whether that easing of the militant tradition may not be in itself a sign of the vast success of adult education over the 150 years of its putative life. This possibility is given muscle by Stevens's own narrative of the Open University, surely our society's very best token of national self-education and democratic access. The name of the great Richard Hoggart as well as that of his magnificent lieutenant, Stuart Hall, serve here to remind us that the point of national education, alongside the necessities of vocational training and making a living, is for each of its citizens to be made capable of finding a usable selfhood. It is then to discover in the fields of knowledge that labour which is not only its own reward, but which permits a student freedom from his or her own limitations.

Phil Stevens has written a book that keeps faith with both his principles and his tradition. A writer can hardly do more. If adult education is, as I suggest here, one of the greatest accomplishments of our national culture and politics, it is the human practice recorded and celebrated in these pages that gives it unquenchable life.

Fred Inglis
Emeritus Professor of Cultural Studies, University of Sheffield

Chapter 1

Introducing a noble tradition

Since the end of the Second World War, British society has changed beyond recognition. Our education system has struggled to keep up with the pace of change. A former colleague once suggested, with some pride, that schools were always 20 years behind developments in society. By nature, educational institutions are conservative places, rooted in tradition and slow to respond to changes in the world around them. This is the case with schools, colleges, and universities where change is usually driven by political imperatives rather than cultural and social developments within the towns and cities they serve.

But there is one area of education that has a proud tradition of leading the way in responding to change. Adult learning has thrown a gentle light on our education system for over two centuries. From modest beginnings in eighteenth-century guilds, Chartism, and non-conformist churches in the north of England, the sector developed through specialist colleges, the trade unions, and the Workers' Educational Association (WEA). Adult education drew its inspiration from reforming Sunday schools, new developments in science and technology, increases in literacy, and the rise of the popular press. The Industrial Revolution drove up literacy levels and provided a strong financial motive for working-class men and women to learn to read and write. If there were utilitarian reasons for workers attending evening classes in the nineteenth century, others had more enquiring minds and were passionate about learning for its own sake. Hundreds of adult students were attracted to subjects such as philosophy, literature, and history, as Jonathan Rose has pointed out in his seminal work on the intellectual life of British workers (Rose, 2001). From the early autodidacts to adult centres and the tutorial classes of the WEA, adults were drawn to intellectual subjects for personal fulfilment, political awareness and a desire to understand the world around them.

From humble beginnings in pit villages across the north of England and south Wales, to church halls and settlement buildings in the East End of London, adult education thrived independently for over a hundred years. In the twentieth century the movement gradually fell into the hands of local authorities or university extension departments where, despite continued threats to its future, it has continued to prosper. From time to time these threats have been self-inflicted. Bitter ideological conflicts down the years have threatened to bring the noble tradition to its knees. The history of adult education is punctuated by political conflict, often bordering on outright hostility that has threatened careers and even the future of institutions themselves.

In the pages that follow we examine these conflicts so we can better understand why adult learning continues to be such a vital, although often contested, part of our culture. Historian Roger Fieldhouse has argued that adult education has developed from a 'movement' into a 'service', losing its central mission along the way (Fieldhouse, 1996). Fieldhouse is only partly right. One of the central arguments of this book is that the founding spirit and purpose of adult learning has survived, despite the trend towards state and bureaucratic control.

Fieldhouse (1996), Brian Simon (1990), and Thomas Kelly (1992) have all produced comprehensive histories of British adult education and it is not my intention to compete with these eminent historians. I am more interested in tracing key developments in the sector through looking in detail at six specialist adult institutions with international reputations for innovation and high standards. Between them they cater for a broad range of adult students from entry level to postgraduate study. The future of adult education depends on how successfully these institutions adapt to a world of constant cultural and social change. What we have found is that an exciting new model of adult education has begun to emerge, specially designed to meet the educational needs of a changing adult demographic.

The book attempts to throw some light into those dark corridors and musty classrooms where adult students flock to study everything from Mandarin Chinese to music appreciation. Today adults turn up to get themselves fit or to learn web design, while others are more interested in taking qualifications that could dramatically change their lives. These pages are a celebration of the remarkable achievements of adult students across the spectrum, from asylum seekers and trafficked people in the inner city, desperately trying to learn a new language and adapt to a new culture, to those recovering from dependency, abuse, or other personal difficulties. At the heart of the adult education movement is a strong sense of thwarted potential and a desire to make a better life. Of course, many adults attend classes simply to have fun or to learn a specific skill or subject. Long may this continue, but the essence of adult learning is about people wanting to change their lives and realize their potential.

The book traces the history of adult education to the present day and looks at current practice through the eyes of a diverse group of students studying at the following institutions: Ruskin College, Birkbeck College, the Open University, the Mary Ward Centre, the Working Men's College, and Harris Manchester College (HMC). For research purposes I initially approached eight major adult education centres in the UK, together with the Open University and HMC, which draw students from across the world. All six of those above responded enthusiastically while the remaining two failed to reply.

All of the partner colleges were full and willing partners in the project, and every student participated voluntarily. Students were invited to submit their educational story and around 250 students made an initial response to notices in college newsletters and websites, or through appeals by staff at each institution. Of the 250 initial respondents, just over 200 joined the project as full participants. Each participant was provided with a set of project guidelines and invited to complete a simple form in which they had the opportunity to outline their educational story, although some preferred a personal interview. The participants had the choice to remain anonymous, although only one student chose not to reveal his or her name. The occasional script was edited and every participant signed off the final version of their story. I eventually received 98 educational autobiographies and they form a major part of the research material for this book. The research followed ethical guidelines within developing relationships of trust and openness. The stories provide a fascinating insight into the motives, aspirations, and experiences of today's adult learners. The students attend or have attended a range of adult programmes from beginners' courses in a range of subjects to highly prized degree programmes.

Restrictions of space meant that I could not look at adult learning in Scotland, Wales, or Northern Ireland, nor in the United States. Further education colleges, although delivering important adult vocational programmes, and the community college movement, wiped out by government cuts, are also outside the scope of this enquiry. Nor is there sufficient space to provide a detailed analysis of the recent explosion of MOOCs (massive online, on-demand, open courses). These are nothing new and we can trace distance learning back to the nineteenth century, as the railways, postal services, and moving pictures developed. In 1962, in the isolation of his prison cell, Nelson Mandela began a distance learning degree from London University that the future President of South Africa completed in 1981.

Now smartphones, tablets, and high-speed internet have transformed the way universities and college think about the delivery of their programmes. MOOCs are a $40 billion business – big bucks indeed. Coursera, the major provider of online course in the United States, claims to have 4.7 million subscribers sourcing courses from 87 universities – again impressive, if these figures are correct.

In the UK, 21 universities have signed up to the government's FutureLearn programme, which provides a variety of free online courses. However, nothing is ever really free and most MOOCs require subscribers to pay for accreditation on completion of their course. There is little doubt that MOOCs will revolutionize conventional models of formal education. But to what extent only time will tell. The high-technology model is not without its problems, which might be serious enough to derail the whole enterprise. Retention rates are low and there is little in the way of personalized or adaptive learning, a problem that has been accepted by the industry. Sebastian Thrun, co-founder of Udacity, one of the world's major providers of online study, admitted his company had a 'lousy product'.

MOOCs seem to work for highly motivated students who are keen to upgrade their vocational skills portfolio. There is little in the way of sympathetic learner support or differentiation in teaching. Pearson, the education company, has invested $9 billion in open-source learning and is determined to rival the quality teaching, student support, and retention rates of conventional providers. We shall see, but although education's tectonic plates are certainly on the move, there is little evidence at this stage that adult students will abandon traditional colleges and universities for the uncertainty of an online education. The Open University has produced distance learning programmes for four decades and has increased its online courses in recent years. It remains to be seen whether the newer providers can match the OU's proven quality.

'Fibre optic', 'downloading', and 'open source' are not part of the vocabulary we traditionally associate with adult learning and its enduring image of cold and draughty classrooms on January evenings, and queues round the block. It is tempting to draw the conclusion that the founding virtues of adult learning – intellectual engagement, the acquisition of knowledge in the pursuit of social justice, and radical theories of teaching that reach back to the late eighteenth century – have been abandoned in favour of individualized online delivery. One of the aims of this book is to show that the old values are alive and well, having survived, even embraced, technological change. If we accept that the history of education is related to social and cultural, and now technological, change, then the challenge to all of those providing adult education remains the same as it was when the Working Men's College was first established in 1854: how to adapt to the different educational needs of each new generation. Both the needs and motives of adult learners change and a further aim here is to identify these changes within a general trend.

In Chapter 2 we follow the educational autobiographies of three engaging autodidacts. The story of a young British POW with a gift for words and a desire to make a better life for himself and his family is heartening and inspirational. Taking advantage of the new opportunities available in adult learning in the 1960s and 1970s, a factory worker gave up the security of a steady job to fulfil his dream of a university education, and if that wasn't enough, became in retirement a highly regarded jazz singer. A young girl left school in the early 1960s with few or no qualifications. In her 20s she obtained a 1st-class degree in the Humanities, enjoyed a successful teaching career, and later in life turned her considerable intelligence to science. In 2014, at the age of 64, she became the proud possessor of a BSc in Geosciences.

Through the stories of a group of students entering adult education for the first time, Chapter 3 examines the rich diversity of programmes on offer at the Mary Ward Centre and the Working Men's College (WMC), both situated in the London Borough of Camden. Each institution has a long and distinguished history of providing second-chance education for adults from largely immigrant communities. One of the central questions raised in Chapter 3 is the extent to which adult learning should be concerned with building communities and helping disadvantaged neighbourhoods, rather than delivering courses in the traditional way. Both the Mary Ward and the WMC have adapted to the modern world with great foresight, forging a new model of adult learning in the process.

Ruskin College demands a special place in any narrative of British adult education. In its own words, Ruskin is a 'flagship, learner-centred sustainable college'. This rather worthy statement tells us little about the essence of the place. Now set on the outskirts of Oxford in the leafy dormitory suburb of Headington, Ruskin is a residential adult college with a unique history. The college accommodates some of the most interesting students currently involved in adult learning. Chapter 4 traces the history of this unique institution and its innovative approach to teaching and learning and examines the experience of today's Ruskin students.

Harris Manchester College (HMC) and Birkbeck College are two of the most highly regarded higher education institutions in the UK. Both HMC and Birkbeck are exclusively for adult students. Harris Manchester is a full Oxford University college and its students are subject to the same rigorous academic standards as every other Oxford student. A college of the University of London, Birkbeck delivers courses almost exclusively in the evenings. Chapter 5 describes the experiences of a group of undergraduates and postgraduates studying at these two prestigious institutions. They are a remarkable group, whose achievements deserve special recognition and respect. The HMC and Birkbeck students sit at the pinnacle of the adult education movement in the UK and follow a long and distinguished line.

Chapter 6 focuses on adult distance learning and in particular the experience of students at the Open University. The response from OU students was overwhelming, with the participants keen to share their fascinating stories, which exemplify the sense of pride, courage, and determination shown by generations of distance learning students. In contrast to our other institutions, the students at the OU are not building-based and do not have the same amount of contact with tutors. Their successes are consequently all the more notable.

The stories that appear in the book from all partner institutions were selected from a group of participants who have studied, or are currently studying, a range of subjects at all levels. The stories afford revealing insights into the students' experience, their motivations, fears, and aspirations. One of the most significant trends in adult learning over the past 30 years has been the dramatic increase in the number of women students in the sector and this is reflected in recruitment figures for all six partners. The multi-ethnic complexity of our inner cities has provided a further challenge to designers of adult learning programmes. Today's adult students believe that success in the classroom begins with feeling secure, free from ridicule and humiliation, and valued. These developments in the sector are a challenge to colleges and their staff in terms of teaching and learning and their sensitivity to the different needs of today's students.

Some of the most interesting issues raised by our participants relate to their school experiences. As long as society in general and schools in particular continue to fail so many of our young people, the argument for adult education is undeniable. Governments repeatedly talk up schools as having the ability to change children's lives for the better, conveniently ignoring the fact that poverty and disadvantage damage children's chances. In a *Guardian* article in 2014, Melissa Benn argued that since 2010 the Coalition government has widened the gap between rich and poor, and:

> I cannot recall a single example ... publicly conceding that poverty has a significant impact on educational outcomes, or admitting the brazen elitism of our school system.

Benn reports that the Organisation for Economic Co-operation and Development (OECD) has stated unequivocally that, 'If education is to make a real difference, fairer school systems have to go hand in hand with policies to enhance economic equality.' In relation to access to higher education, the educational charity the Sutton Trust confirms Benn's view about the relation between social class and success at school: 'The main driver of inequality in access to university remains the stubborn link between attainment at school and family background.' (Sutton Trust press release, 27 July 2014).

The Trust also reveals that in the academic year 2011–12 the five top private schools supplied as many entrants to Oxford and Cambridge universities as all of the 1,800 state schools that also send pupils to Oxbridge. The evidence of elitism and inequality is overwhelming. This is despite state schools having improved significantly over the past 30 years. In the 1950s and early 1960s teachers were often harsh, aloof, even brutal. Many of the participants in the research recall enduring violence, abuse, and humiliation at schools in both the state and private sectors. However, if teachers today are more understanding and supportive of young people, all of their hard work is in danger of being squandered.

Introducing selection by stealth for 11 year olds, removing schools from local accountability and thus inviting inherent problems of compromised leadership, irresponsible governance, and potentially corrupt financial management – these are leading to a fragmented school system designed to reward the rich and sharp-elbowed middle class at the expense of the poor and vulnerable. Tory governments beef up the private sector, introduce innovations such as the ridiculously named 'free schools', reintroduce linear examinations, and push through a school curriculum that denies the multicultural nature of British society while promoting a misty-eyed nationalism. Given such unashamedly divisive measures in schools and with so many working-class men and women in alienating jobs on poverty-level wages and zero-hours contracts, adult education is as important today as it was in the mid-nineteenth century.

The students' stories in these pages reveal that the desire to learn remains deeply embedded in thousands of adult students, young and old, across the country. The stories demonstrate that people will go to the most extraordinary lengths to make up for lost time. Of course, it would be wrong to argue for adult education solely on the grounds of inadequate schooling. Many people succeed in life having left school without qualifications, contrary to the thoughts of some of our more evangelistic adult educators. Some make a good living as plumbers, carpenters, or care workers, or become successful in business. But, as our narrative histories suggest, although an appreciable number of adults are thirsty to learn and acquire knowledge, many of them were denied the opportunity at school.

Like all areas of academic life, adult learning has not escaped the clutches of theory. In Britain, along with Edward Thompson, Richard Hoggart and Raymond Williams directed their formidable minds to issues around teaching and learning in adult education. All were socialist thinkers and viewed adult education, and education more generally, as a means of liberating individuals and achieving social justice. In the 1970s the Brazilian educationalist Paulo Freire made his own theoretical intervention, which has probably enjoyed more lasting influence. From a revolutionary tradition, the Brazilian's *Pedagogy of the Oppressed* (1972) has directly influenced curriculum planning and approaches to teaching adults, particularly in our inner cities, as we shall see.

Freire's emphasis on dialogue between teachers and students struck an influential chord with adult educators working with marginalized communities. Less structured and more flexible learning opportunities in the form of dialogue or conversation between an institution and its community is claimed to be far more liberating than simply offering a conventional programme. Freire insisted that any dialogue between educators and their community should be governed by the notion of respect. The adult curriculum should evolve through discussion, with educators and students listening to each other and working together. Freire uses the metaphor of 'banking' to describe much of what counts as formal education, quite an interesting metaphor given the history of our financial institutions over the past ten years. In this argument, bits of knowledge are simply 'deposited' in individual minds to be withdrawn at some future point, a view that has little to do with education in any acceptable sense.

For Freire, education should make a difference to the world. We will see how centres such as Mary Ward and the Working Men's College in London aim to build social capacity in their communities in the interests of social justice. This notion of adult education for community development and change differs from the nineteenth-century objectives of social harmony or giving working-class men improved skills in the interests of a more efficient workforce. Freire's insistence on contextualizing adult learning in the lived experience of students opened a whole range of possibilities for the way informal educators operate. His influence continues to resonate in the new model of learning we find in adult centres up and down the country today. Because of its enduring relevance, Freire's liberation model has outlived that of the more industrial, class-based ideal exemplified by the work of Williams, Thompson, Hoggart, and teacher-philosophers such as Raphael Samuel.

Objections to Freire's philosophy of education tend to rest on his reifying everyday experience. This is simply not how teachers work. In my own experience of over 30 years in adult education, students don't usually want to be reminded of their disadvantages or the perceived poverty of their own experience. They are keen to learn, acquire knowledge, and be introduced to exciting new ideas and do not want to look back. Of course, some need to improve their language skills or be taught to use a computer, but the point remains. The notion of dialogue set against a predefined curriculum is admirable, but it is only a partial view of adult learning. There are also epistemological problems to do with how collective learning works and whether communities can be educated in any real sense, but these are outside the scope of this enquiry. Good teachers will look for 'teachable moments' where they can relate an idea to everyday life, but it is not always possible to use lived experience as a starting point. Teachers are expected to teach.

A second objection to Freire's revolutionary thinking rests on a diluted theory of indoctrination. A teacher could simply smuggle his or her own ideas and values into the class under the guise of neutrality. Taylor argues that Freire's philosophy of education falls down because:

> The rhetoric which announced the importance of dialogue, engagement, and equality, and denounced silence ... and oppression, did not match in practice the subliminal messages and modes of a Banking System of education. Albeit benign, Freire's approach differs only in degree, but not in kind, from the system which he so eloquently criticizes.
>
> (Taylor, 1993: 148)

Despite these criticisms, Freire's ideas continue to attract teachers and curriculum planners sensitive to injustices and inequalities in our society. The great theorists of adult learning share a common assumption: that education and politics are inextricably linked. In this view, the prevailing political ideology will determine the type of education on offer. Conservative secretaries of state bully our schools into an ideological return to the 1950s, religious leaders use schools to promote their faith, and socialists and liberationists see adult education as part of the struggle for social justice. Opposing sets of political philosophies reflect sharp divisions in our society that spill over into outright hostility with regard to the aims and purposes of education. The defence of Williams, Thompson, Hoggart, and Freire is based on the premise that adult learning should be part of the complex process of building an educated democracy, and not just about the allocation of scarce resources or political interference. It goes to the heart of a democratic philosophy of education – the relationship between teaching and learning. With echoes of Freire's thinking, Raymond Williams puts it this way:

> Education is a two-way process – teachers must learn from those they teach and culture is what men and women make it: its bedrock is the decencies which make it possible for people to live together in education and society.
>
> (Williams, 1999: 1)

All of the authors referred to above share Williams's robust defence of adult learning and their ideas will be more fully explored in what follows. Thousands of adults share this view. Utilitarian outcomes are real but for most adult students they are secondary to the actual process of learning for its own sake. This is a deeply democratic idea and a vital element in the constant battle for social justice and human dignity for the marginalized, dispossessed, and discouraged in our society. Williams once said that we must be eternally vigilant in the face of reaction against hard-won social and political gains. His observation is as relevant today as it was when he was writing in the mid-1970s.

Recent thinking and research has centred less on the learning experience than the so-called 'impact' of adult learning. In his blog, 'Demonstrating the social purpose impact of adult education', Peter Caldwell, WEA Director of Curriculum Planning, describes 'social purpose' as:

> How people's life chances can be transformed and society changed and developed in a more democratic, equal and cohesive basis.
>
> (Caldwell, 2013)

Caldwell lists the outcomes of a 'social purpose' definition of adult learning as 'health and well-being, employability, community engagement and culture'. Taken together, these four blockbuster 'themes' should form the basis of a new pedagogy and the structure of a revised curriculum. These 'themes', Caldwell claims, are best applied to 'inner-city struggles around housing, regeneration and community'. The WEA blogger also emphasizes the importance of embedded study skills and developing students' powers of critical thinking, as this was something radically different from the practice of the past 30 years.

In her slim volume, Carrie Birch (2013) draws on individual life histories of adult students to make connections between social and educational inequalities in the UK. Birch's research, the first of a series of papers by the National Institute of Adult Continuing Education (NIACE) on the impact of adult education, confirms that poverty is an obstacle to educational opportunity within disadvantaged communities. From this patently obvious point, Birch argues that policymakers should be made aware of the impact that adult learning could have in regenerating these communities. Health and well-being, investment, economic growth, and productivity are all possible positive impacts of adult learning in deprived communities or, as Birch repeatedly describes people living in inner-city housing estates, the 'socially excluded' – a fashionable term among sociologists that refers to people living in poverty and inadequate housing, whose children attend underfunded and demoralized schools, and whose ability to influence change for the better is pretty much zero.

Caldwell and Birch's research on the social impact of adult learning adds little to what we already know, although Caldwell's continued dialogue on curriculum ideas and Birch's use of 'narrative histories' in her research are welcome. Some of their radical ideas have been applied in places like the Mary Ward Centre and the Working Men's College for at least 20 years and we see examples in later chapters of this book. In their different ways, Birch and Caldwell repeat Paulo Freire and Raymond Williams's demands made over 30 years ago for a negotiated pedagogy where students have greater control over curriculum planning. Despite these reservations, it can only be a good thing that adult learning continues to be the subject of research and critical attention at a time when the venomous ideological attack on public expenditure has reached crisis point.

In 2013, adult learning was added to the victim list of the government's cost-cutting austerity measures. The Skills Funding Statement of that year announced a crippling 19 per cent reduction in the adult skills budget by 2015–16. The statement also confirmed the decision to scrap loans for apprenticeships for young adults. These punitive measures are compounded by severe cuts in local authority funding, to the point where adult learning has ceased to exist in many areas of the country. This is nothing new. The sector has been in perpetual crisis for 200 years, as the experience of Mary Ward and George Birkbeck reminds us. As always, we need to fight for it. Some will argue that cuts in the adult learning budget are defensible. They will tell you that the 'historic mission of adult education is over'. With improved schooling, more opportunities in higher education, and better vocational training, everybody has his or her chance. This view takes no account of the millions of young people and adults who, for one reason or another, are let down by the system. Therefore, we should be encouraged that, in spite of seemingly insurmountable obstacles, thousands of courageous adults seek a haven in libraries, colleges, and universities, and continue to fight against the odds to fulfil their potential and achieve a better life. With austerity Britain hitting the poor the hardest, our political leaders ignore W.B. Yeats's appeal for compassion:

> But I, being poor, have only my dreams;
> I have spread my dreams under your feet;
> Tread softly because you tread on my dreams.
>
> (Yeats, 'Aedh Wishes for the Cloths of Heaven')

If one of the purposes of this book is to stimulate a debate about the aims and objectives of adult learning, a related aim is to promote and celebrate a vital and liberating part of our culture, often regarded as the Cinderella of our education system. Most tutors and college staff who contributed to the research for the book argue that political and social justice should be the primary aims of adult learning. Only a handful of the 200-plus adult students interviewed in the research saw their decision to study in this way. So we have a contrast in the way providers and their students view the aims of adult education, something we explore in later chapters. Philosophy and theory are important in defining aims and objectives and help to clarify our thinking, but the essence of the book is the stories of human dignity and flourishing of people who have reached higher and changed their lives through their own efforts, aided by adult educators who have a passionate belief in the special nature of their work.

Chapter 2

Lowering voices and raising minds

For centuries, working people have expressed a desire to learn. For most of his life the early nineteenth-century labourer-poet John Clare was obsessed with the need to know and learn. I have an 'itching for everything,' he declared. In a poem to the memory of his old schoolteacher, Clare wrote:

> This little learning which I now enjoy, a gift so dear that nothing can destroy.

> (Bate, 2003)

The former agricultural labourer's pursuit of knowledge took him out of poverty in rural Northamptonshire on his journey to become one of the greatest poets in the English language. Clare's story is exceptional. Others, from equally modest backgrounds and similar dreams, failed to flourish in the manner of John Clare.

Thomas Hardy's fictional character Jude Fawley, who aspires to Oxford University but is destined to remain a simple stonemason, is arguably the most eloquent illustration of ordinary people's obsession with learning, so passionately expressed by John Clare. Inspired by his schoolmaster, Jude sets out with grim determination to learn Greek and Latin – the subjects he will need for university entrance. But his dream of a 'Christminster' education ends in disappointment as the author brings the Wessex dreamer abruptly down to earth. Jude is a classic Hardy tragic figure and the author is brutally honest in denying the young orphan from rural Dorset his fantasy of a university education. Hardy's social criticism reveals itself in *Jude the Obscure* – the working-class Fawley has intellectual pretensions but society is bound to frustrate them. Writing in the late nineteenth century, Hardy accepts the cerebral instincts of working-class people such as Fawley, but, unlike John Clare, he believes their aspirations will remain unfulfilled.

This instinct and desire for knowledge among common people is often juxtaposed by nineteenth-century authors to a more formal education. In the novels of Hardy and Charles Dickens, particularly in the latter's anti-utilitarian work *Hard Times,* formal education is set against the social values of community and neighbourhood. Both writers see education as a barrier, not an opportunity, for working people. Raymond Williams used the individualist metaphor of the 'ladder' to characterize the British education system in the twentieth century. Those who are successful in the system go up the 'ladder' one at a time, often pulling it up beneath them. Following Dickens and Hardy, Williams sets educated values against those of the working class. In this view, nineteenth-century education thwarted the natural instincts and intellectual ambitions of ordinary people who have always valued learning, but not necessarily in a formalized setting.

Gradually, in the eighteenth and nineteenth centuries, an alternative to formal education began to emerge. This took two forms: autodidactism, exemplified by Clare, and the self-help movement of mutual and improvement societies. There was always a close link between these two forms of adult learning, particularly with the advent of free public libraries in the late nineteenth century. But, like John Clare, most autodidacts remained fiercely independent. They were literate individuals who took their learning from whatever came to hand, including cheap editions of Shakespeare, Milton, and most of the classic Greek texts. Workers such as the Chartist Thomas Cooper, who had mastered Shakespeare, Plato, and Euclid by the age of 24, devoured everything they could lay their hands on. Historian Edward Thompson acknowledged the heroic efforts of these extraordinary people, arguing that working-class autodidacts were partly responsible for the 'planting of the liberty tree' in the early nineteenth century, inhabiting, 'every town and in many villages throughout England'. (Thompson, 1968: 201)

With a shelf full of radical books, the autodidact came from every area of working-class life. Their learning, Thompson argued, 'was their own'. Many like the trade union leader John Burns had deprived themselves and their families of food to buy books and papers (Fieldhouse, 2001: 12). Burns was the sixteenth child of a poor, one-parent family from south London and his mother worked tirelessly to keep her enormous family housed and fed. There is a striking engraving in Cassell's *Illustrated History of England* in which Burns is pictured addressing a large group of London dock workers around the time of the 1889 'dockers' tanner' strike. Burns had a national reputation as a great orator and his speeches were an inspiration to thousands of London's dock workers. He was also a prodigious reader determined to make sense of the rapidly changing world around him.

In addition to helping London dockers with his well-respected negotiating skills, Burns was an active member of the Socialist Democratic Federation (SDF) and founder of the party's Battersea Branch. In February 1887, the south Londoner was the keynote speaker at a socialist rally in Trafalgar Square that ended in chaos, culminating in police baton charges and hundreds of injured protesters. Along with several of his fellow organizers, Burns was found guilty of incitement charges and sentenced to six weeks in prison – he was just 25 years old. A few weeks in Pentonville failed to dampen either Burns's intellectual passion or his enthusiasm for radical politics. This formidable individual was elected MP for Battersea in 1892, where he sat on the opposition benches close to another distinguished new member, Keir Hardie. Burns's persistence and outstanding analytical abilities later earned him a place in the Cabinet, where he excelled at the Board of Trade. At the end of his long career devoted to the socialist movement, Burns retired to his books and his beloved cricket.

Burns was arguably the most distinguished of the nineteenth-century autodidacts, but there were many others who found a way to educate themselves in spite of poor and inadequate schooling. Among them was the radical socialist, soldier, and policeman John Pearman. Born in 1819, Pearman was also brought up in extreme poverty. But unlike the great orators, he expressed his learning not through political activity or splendid oratory, but in his writing. Pearman's working-class autobiography, *Memoir*, was based on his policeman's notebook and provides a fascinating account of his life and emerging ideas on politics and social justice. As Carolyn Steedman argues (1989), there is little doubt that Pearman's writing skills were acquired in adulthood. Steedman argues that he wrote his way to political consciousness:

> The individual struggle of many 19th century working people must have been to free themselves from the official hopelessness that every legitimized trajectory of thought presented them with … I am pleased to think that he freed himself from this particular crippling doctrine.

For Steedman, the writer/policeman confronted 'a written history that showed the poor and lowly that they occupied a proper and divinely ordered place'. In his typical and unpunctuated style, Pearman set out to expose privilege and injustice as he saw it:

> When I look back for only the past two generations of my family what an amount of temptations we have to endure or avoid to look at if what our persons calls sin to git a chance to live while our Queen and the Lords and Dukes fare of the best the poor children of this carrupt earth can get for them … there is one Law for the poor and another for the rich.
>
> (ibid.)

Pearman is clearly writing from speech, but he is also writing his way to political understanding. This 'intellectual leap of understanding', to use Steedman's phrase, enables Pearman to set his own personal experience and that of his family within a general criticism of society. Whether his political understanding came from the practice of writing or from personal observation is a moot point. His *Memoir* provides us with an invaluable account of working-class consciousness in the nineteenth century. His erudition and learning owe nothing to education in the conventional sense, itself an indication of the magnitude of his achievement.

John Burns and John Pearman were self-taught, working-class men who dreamed of a better world – Burns through political activism, while our policeman preferred close social observation, which he expressed in his writing. In reading rooms, public libraries, and village halls across the country, nineteenth-century working-class intellectuals such as Burns and Pearman devoted themselves to hours of learning and study. As Roger Fieldhouse remarked, their 'sacrifice and devotion is unquestioned' (Fieldhouse, 2001: 12).

What was all this hard-won learning for? Was it self-realization that the education system had failed them, religious understanding, a passionate desire for knowledge, or simply a burning desire to be part of the revolutionary transformation of their time? The answer is a mixture of all these things, and their learning almost certainly had a strong social purpose. But one thing is clear: the nineteenth-century autodidacts were not striving to become members of the aspiring middle classes, but steadfastly remained true to their working-class roots. These near-heroic figures were instrumental in creating a new working-class culture based on a love of learning and a desire for self-improvement. To what extent this nineteenth-century proletarian enthusiasm for knowledge and learning has survived will be a question for later chapters.

The passion these dedicated individuals had for reading has been interpreted by some to be a slavish, almost biblical devotion to the text and an associated inability to think independently. This is at best ungenerous and at worst insulting and betrays a lack of understanding of the reality of working-class life and culture. As Raymond Williams claimed, 'culture is ordinary'. In other words, a love of ideas, debate, and enquiry was deeply ingrained in the valleys of Welsh mining communities, the pits of Yorkshire and Derbyshire, and the cotton mills of Lancashire. Judgement and criticism were not exclusively the preserve of the educated bourgeois class. It is patronizing to assume that great works are not for the likes of working people. Why wouldn't they be?

Later in the nineteenth century the autodidactic tradition began to be absorbed into improvement societies, fellowship groups, and socialist guilds with their evening classes, study weekends, and Sunday schools. With the expansion of more organized adult learning, scholarly individuals could now find their voice in the company of other, like-minded souls. The collective form of adult education as it emerged in the early twentieth century with the Workers' Educational Association (WEA) began to resemble what we recognize today. However, as the WEA and other independent providers were incorporated into the state system, their more radical intentions were diffused. The process of incorporation failed to deter the most determined, and the flame of this noble tradition continued to burn brightly in a few free-thinking individuals, well into the twentieth century. The following is the story of a courageous individual who, in a time of war, doggedly pursued a path to knowledge and understanding, but never lost sight of Hardy's 'customary values' or Clare's 'gift so dear'.

From our own correspondent

Like many of his generation, Jack Stevens was self-taught. Public libraries and life experience provided the crucible of his education. He was in the very best tradition of mid-twentieth-century autodidacts and a habitual letter writer. The editor of the local paper received a constant stream of letters from J.D. Stevens on some road safety matter or a local issue in his role as secretary of his local branch of the National Painters' Society. These frequently published missives are well written, confident in tone, and show a real civic concern. In a letter published in the *Walthamstow Guardian*, our correspondent rages gently against the growing practice of DIY and its effects on local tradespeople. His writing is full of rhetorical flourishes and neat turns of phrase:

> ... have another string to your bow by all means, but don't imagine you can conduct a symphony orchestra (I don't know, perhaps that was Sir Malcolm driving that 38 bus after all).
>
> (*Walthamstow Guardian*, 10 May 1951)

The letter is well argued and full of imagery and metaphor. These are the jottings of a working man from a humble background who endured the most basic pre-war schooling east London had to offer. The erudition surfaced in spite of his limited education and, like many people then and since, Jack's learning began in earnest once he left full-time education. Libraries, the radio, the *Reynolds' News*, and his trade union work formed his curriculum and provided his teaching. The peaceful setting of the public library provided a rich resource for a young and enquiring mind in the late 1930s, together with a warm and comfortable place to write letters. But that secure and reassuring world was to be shattered by events happening on the other side of Europe. The outbreak of war in 1939 changed things for ever for people like Jack Stevens. The experience of war brutalized daily life and brought years of hardship and tragedy. Ironically, as we shall see, one of the most decisive influences on Jack's learning was probably his war years spent incarcerated in a German prison camp hidden deep in a Polish forest.

Figure 1: A young Jack Stevens captured in a drawing by a German POW just after the war in 1945.

Jack was a prisoner of war between 1943 and 1945. Nothing exceptional about that: thousands of young British combatants were captured and imprisoned during the Second World War, held for years in subhuman conditions and subjected to the cruel barbarism of the Nazi regime. They were mostly in their 20s, with young families back in the UK. When Jack was posted abroad in the winter of 1942, his young wife was five months' pregnant. I have in my possession a copy of the list of British POWs at Stalag VIIIB at Lamsdorf – the Germans were meticulous record-keepers. One page of the document contains a list of over 80 prisoners by the name of Stevens; there are a similar number under the name of Stephens. In addition to this distressingly long register there is a single page for each POW that includes name, rank, number, home address, details of capture, and a smudged fingerprint. The most harrowing image on the page for Jack Stevens is a grainy photograph of a shaven-headed, gaunt young man, staring into the distance in bewilderment, facing a reality of privation and indignity.

One January day in 1941, Jack walked into the army recruitment centre at Whipps Cross Hospital in east London and signed up for the duration of the war. Following initial training in Edinburgh, the 24-year-old coachman from Walthamstow was posted to North Africa with the 3rd Battalion Grenadier Guards. His unit arrived in Algeria in November 1942 and was quickly pressed into service in the fierce fighting characteristic of the early North Africa campaign. One searingly hot day, after being subjected to hours of relentless enemy fire, Jack's unit became isolated. Facing certain death they surrendered to the Italian forces. This terrifying experience had a profound effect on the men battling to defend a random hill in the middle of the African desert. Such are the vagaries of war that Jack and his fellow soldiers exchanged the baking hot African desert for a freezing Eastern European forest.

There is little doubt that being captured and removed from the action had a profound psychological effect on the POWS and Stevens was no exception, although like most that lived through the experience he rarely talked about it. The desire for learning is fulfilled in a myriad of different ways. Some take up formal learning opportunities to change their lives, others use life itself as the crucible for their learning. Midge Gillies, in her moving account of the lives of POWs in the Second World War, *The Barbed-Wire University* (2012), touches on the noble tradition of self-education in the context of war. Gillies paints a bleak picture of what life was like for Allied prisoners. She writes, 'For most … there were no heroic escapes through secret tunnels ... the reality was a constant battle against boredom and brutality' (Gillies, 2012).

Many POWs tried to escape and a few succeeded – their stories are well documented. But most found the courage to cope through what Gillies describes as 'mental escape', as she explains:

> their bravery is of a different kind ... of keeping going through the everyday boredom and uncertainty of life as a POW ... the men who stole back time from their captors through creativity.
>
> (ibid.: xvi)

These prisoners concealed their 'quiet desperation' in creative activities – organizing theatrical productions, lectures, debates, and sporting events. Tailors, costume designers, academics, painters, singers, musicians, and professional sportsmen combined to produce performances that cheered the hearts and elevated the minds of these sad young men. Gillies research shows us that the men:

> set up universities, became experienced actors and musicians ... sat exams, studied birds, wrote books and poetry and made lasting friendships that crossed class and nationality.
>
> (ibid.: xix)

It helped that some POWS were talented artists and actors in their own right. Among the hundreds of POWs at Stalag VIIIB were the actor Denholm Elliott and Terry Frost, the great abstract artist later knighted for his outstanding contribution to British painting. Elliott, a wireless operator who was shot down on his first mission, had his hands tied in front of his body with Red Cross string used to tie prisoners' parcels, as were most prisoners. Later the string was replaced by iron manacles.

Terry Frost played a full part in the various activities staged at Lamsdorf. A useful high jumper, Frost joined in the sports organized by the prisoners who, as Frost observed, were endlessly imaginative. He remembered:

> There was nobody who wasn't wanted, like Smudger Smith who ... was the greatest manufacturer of a kitchen stove to boil the water to cook the meals in and to make the booze.
>
> (ibid.: 83)

Corporal Terry Frost made his own brushes while in captivity from metal cut from cocoa tins and any bits of wood he could find. He made his paint by mixing oil from sardine cans. The ever-resourceful artist picked flowers as the subject for a still life and became acutely aware of his surroundings – he used his wartime experience to develop his unique aesthetic. Like Jack Stevens, Frost was captured by the Italians, but in the depths of the Ethiopian jungle rather than on a remote desert outcrop. The colours, shapes, and landscape of Africa later inspired Frost's vibrant abstract paintings. There is little doubt, as Gillies suggests, that his African experience 'sharpened his sense and gave him a new landscape'.

The sheer boredom of Stalag life drove people like Frost and Elliott to enliven their existence, and those of others, by performing, painting, and playing sport. Camp debating societies included lively topics such as: 'Has youth too much to say for itself?', ' Is capital punishment justified?', and 'Theatre versus cinema'. Musical productions, poetry readings, and debating societies not only helped to relieve boredom but provided a valuable educational experience. Terry Frost later described his camp as, 'a university, where he found a pleasure in reading and listening to music and poetry' (ibid.).

Given his intellectual and political interests, there is no question that Jack Stevens would have played a full part in all of the activities made available in Stalag VIIIB. He had a lively, enquiring mind and would have relished the opportunity to participate fully in POW 'university' life. It may seem odd, even bizarre, to describe prison camps as educational institutions, but for young men like Stevens, Terry Frost, and hundreds of others, camp life was a learning experience, if a painful one. It was something they could never forget. Jack returned home after the war a better-educated young man and free of the bitterness you might expect after three years detached from his family deep in a Silesian forest.

When the hostilities ceased, the Lamsdorf prisoners were free at last. They were an extraordinary group of young men. They may have been starving, cold, and frightened that they'd never see their loved ones again, but their spirit was never broken as they demonstrated on their perilous homeward journey across Europe. Jack Stevens was repatriated on 29 May 1945 and released to the Reserve in September 1946. The Guardsman was reunited with his family in June 1945.

When L. Cpl Stevens arrived home he had lost over four stones in captivity and was badly undernourished. He was provided with double rations to build up his strength, but his stomach reacted badly to this sudden onslaught and it was some months before he could tolerate the post-war diet. Perhaps missing the comradeship of his fellow prisoners, Jack found it very difficult to settle into normal civilian life. It may not have helped the transition from POW to regular husband and father that the experience of those lost years in the Silesian wilderness remained sealed in his memory. In the days before post-traumatic stress disorder (PTSD), returning prisoners were expected to return to their 'normal' lives with a stiff upper lip and a 'get on with it' mentality. Jack did 'get on with it', but at what cost to his mental well-being we shall never know.

With the war over, people began to rebuild a war-torn and poverty-stricken country. In his documentary film *Spirit of '45*, Ken Loach celebrates a time when British people came together to make a new society, an astonishing endeavour, as Loach's film shows us. They thanked Churchill for his heroic efforts through the war and for standing up to the biggest bully of the twentieth century, and moved towards a different politics. Nothing could be the same again, as Loach reminds us: '1945 was a pivotal year in British history. The unity that carried Britain through the war allied to the bitter memories of the inter-war years led to a vision of a better society.' (Loach, 2013).

After the war, British people yearned for change and expectations were understandably high. For Jack Stevens and his generation, the experience of war sharpened their political focus. At last their hopes and concerns had a genuine voice and they were not to be denied. In 1945 Clem Attlee won a substantial mandate for social and political change and his administration set about its task with revolutionary zeal. Nye Bevan established the NHS and within a few years the Welfare State was fully up and running. However, in education the Labour leaders' traditionalist instincts betrayed them. Despite Attlee's impressive majority, his government lacked the nerve and political courage to rid the country of the class-based system that was rooted in the inequalities of the nineteenth century. Grammar schools survived and public schools prospered. This muddle of a compromise set the pattern of education for the next 60 years. Secondary education was split into a tripartite system of grammar, technical, and secondary modern schools. Performance in the 11+ determined whether a child progressed to the local grammar school or was banished to the blackboard jungle of the secondary modern.

For Jack, with some stability in his life at last, the terrifying experience of North Africa and Stalag VIIIB began to recede into his memory. He resumed his duties as secretary of his local trade union branch, wrote his correspondence, and returned with relish to the sanctuary of the local library and his books. In spite of everything, or maybe because of it, his love of learning remained undiminished. His university was no longer a freezing hut in the middle of Poland, but his local branch library.

Mark Twain once remarked that 'a public library is the most enduring of memorials'. The writer and academic Rita Mae Brown wrote, 'When I got my library card, that's when my life began.' This might seem an exaggerated claim, but those who have spent a lifetime in and around libraries know exactly what Brown means. Libraries have been called 'necessities of life', while rock star Frank Zappa proclaimed, 'If you want an education – go to a library.' Many writers, scholars, and self-educated people will agree with these sentiments about our public libraries. In his evocative poem 'The Library', Richard Armour writes, 'Here is where people, One frequently finds, Lower their voices And raise their minds.'

Jorge Luis Borges regarded libraries as a kind of paradise. I have spent most of my life in institutions with libraries at their heart. But for me, like Jack Stevens, the public library opened up the world. There were few books in the family home, but the rich resources of the library were freely available and open to all. In 1824 Joseph Howe believed that 'poverty of purse cannot exclude' people from public libraries. The novelist Sholem Asch 'simply loved them'. For some, access to a library became a real need, as Jonathan Rose illustrates in his story about a Nottingham dressmaker whose mother found sanctuary in her local library:

> The public library was her salvation. She read four or five books
> a week all her life but had no one to discuss them with. She had
> read all the classics several times over ... the library had a job to
> keep her supplied with current publications.
>
> (Rose, 2001: 5)

Rose's central premise is that working-class readers are as likely to enjoy the great works of literature as their expensively educated 'betters' and sets about providing evidence for his thesis. For ordinary people, a local library was a precondition for access to the classics, although book stalls on market days offered enthusiastic self-educators cheap copies of a wide variety of literature. The popularity of the new libraries was a sign that life was beginning to improve for most Londoners after the horror of the war years. Jack and his wife, an ordinary, working-class young couple living on a local authority housing estate with their seven children, were both prodigious readers. The armfuls of volumes the couple brought home from the library resemble a WEA literature class reading list – Mrs Stevens was a great lover of the Elizabethan period and the historical novels of the New York novelist Anya Seton. She devoured the works of Wilkie Collins,

Catherine Cookson, and Mary Wesley with great relish. The couple were almost certainly familiar with Dickens, Hardy, and Lawrence, while A.J. Cronin, John Braine, and Alan Sillitoe were popular choices each Friday evening. They were keen observers of the 'Lady Chatterley' trial, a moral battle between liberal humanitarianism and what Orwell described as, 'the dead hand of the striped-trousered ones who rule'. A copy of Lawrence's controversial classic soon made its way into the Stevens household.

The list of those who have taught themselves without the guidance of teachers, tutors, or formal institutions is long and distinguished. John Clare, George Bernard Shaw, Ernest Hemingway, and Terry Pratchett all became world-famous writers, but lacked a formal education. The artist John Martin was a nineteenth-century coach painter who had little in the way of formal education, yet his work was the subject of a show at Tate Britain in 2013. Today, aspiring adults can sign up for college courses as mature students with a view to changing their lives. But Jack Stevens was one of those old-style autodidacts who never really aspired to greater things. He acquired his learning through his war experience, the fellowship of his trade union work, and his regular reading. With seven children, working six days a week, attending meetings, reading his daily newspaper, and writing his correspondence, not forgetting ballroom dancing three nights a week, how could he possibly think about a new career or dramatically changing his life? It would never have occurred to him. For individuals like Jack the motivation to learn came from a burning desire to understand the world around them, not to be a great writer or artist. Jack was fine with his life, but wanted to retain some sense of pride in being both a skilled manual worker and an intelligent individual playing a full part in the events round him. People like Jack were true autodidacts who loved learning purely for its own sake – perhaps it was something peculiar to the immediate post-war generation.

Jack died suddenly at the age of 53. He had unfinished business. The children were beginning to flee the nest and at long last he had the space to breathe and think. In many ways his education was only just beginning. Both John Clare and Thomas Hardy would have understood Jack's instinctive desire to know and learn and recognize the obstacles that stood in his way. The readers of Jack's local paper would have missed his regular, compassionate, and erudite letters, which livened their weekend reading.

Diamond geezer

Malcolm Williams let nothing stand in his way. Like Jack Stevens, Williams was a soldier – his age group was the last to be called up for National Service, which he spent either stuck in Catterick or, ironically given his later political views, defending the last of the British Empire out in the Far East. His service experience was very different from those who served in wartime, but at the age of 18 there is no question that the army helped to shape his character and outlook on life. Walthamstow-born Will, as he was known in the east London 'manor' where he grew up, was born in 1938. Not quite a baby boomer, but still able to experience the liberating mood of the 1960s. The Williams family home was a bus ride away from central London and the pubs and clubs of the East End. Will's parents, Jack and Con, were simple working-class folk who lived in a good house in a quiet street close to the shops and local bus routes. Jack and Con welcomed Will's friends to the house with the habitual cup of tea prepared dutifully by mum or his sister, Pauline. Will's dad worked as a fitter at the British Oxygen factory just a couple of miles along the North Circular Road.

Will failed the 11+, something he more than made up for in later life. He worked hard at school and excelled in history and PE, but like most young people attending the local secondary modern, Will left with no qualifications or expectations for the future. On leaving school, the 15 year old worked for a time at the local cork factory, along with dozens of other school leavers from the area. Perhaps the attraction of the cork factory for Will, as a young sports lover, was that the firm made the famous Chingford cricket balls – there seemed no other reason why a bright young lad would take such a dull job. Of course, all boys of Will's age knew they faced National Service just a few years after leaving school. The factory job would pass the time for a couple of years and so it proved.

Will was duly called up and sent to join the Royal Corps of Signals for initial training. Following a short spell in the UK, his regiment was transferred to Malaysia, where they were involved in a few skirmishes defending the local radio station. Will was determined to enjoy army life and he spoke about it with a mixture of fondness and anger. Unlike Jack Stevens, he was happy to talk about his army experience. The two years he spent in the armed forces left a deep impression on the young Londoner and, like his factory experience, contributed greatly to his emerging political consciousness.

A return to civilian life and familiar surroundings in 1956 came as a relief to the 20 year old. Jobs were plentiful and most firms welcomed applications from returning service personnel. Will chose to work at Gestetner, a copy-machine manufacturer in Tottenham. He was determined to be as far away from the cork factory as possible. The new firm was two bus rides away from home and housed in a bleak industrial unit on the Tottenham Marshes. I am sure the only reason he took the job was because the factory was a just short walk from White Hart Lane, home of Will's beloved Spurs football club. A couple of years later he left the Tottenham firm and joined his dad at the British Oxygen Company (BOC), just a few minutes' bike ride away from his parents' house and even closer to the Spurs ground. Will stayed at BOC for the next ten years, gaining the respect of his workmates and earning enough money to buy himself a second-hand Ford Consul. The car was his pride and joy and made him instantly recognizable – not always to his advantage.

Malcolm Williams was a sports fanatic. If his passion was White Hart Lane and the great Spurs side of the early Sixties, he was very active in the local football scene. Such was his enthusiasm for football that Will took his Football Association coaching awards so that he could work in schools and youth clubs – a welcome escape from the mind-numbing drudgery of factory work. With his coaching badge proudly sewn onto his tracksuit, Will accepted a part-time job at Daneford School in Hackney working with top coaches such as Dave Jones and John Cartwright. When he took his Hackney District side to the final of the English Schools Trophy, Jones suggested that Will apply for a teacher-training course. That was just the encouragement he needed.

Will was a hugely popular local 'face'. He was a stocky figure, a little on the short side, with a sleek moustache and always immaculately dressed in his tonic mohair suits and Crombie overcoat. He had a good grasp of Cockney rhyming slang and employed it with relish and a twinkle in his eye. He appeared happy and content, fully integrated back into local life following his military service. But despite his popularity, his girlfriends, and his football, there was something missing. He hadn't forgotten something his tutor had told him back in his army days and it gnawed away at him. Let Will's great friend, Sebastian Coe, tell the story:

> For Malcolm his Damascene moment came when his army tutor asked why he had left school so young, 'because you're quite bright and you're completely wasted here'.
>
> (Coe, 2012: 171)

The tutor made Will promise he would make something of his life when he left the army. If you had attended a rundown secondary modern school, with its disgruntled and cynical teachers, to hear someone say you were bright would have been like a bolt from the blue. It's difficult to overstate the significance of such a remark to someone who by his own admission said, 'Until then, I'd assumed I was a bit dim, like everyone else who lived in our street.'

His tutor's remarks remained with him for many years before he had finally had enough of factory life. He needed to change his life. But how? Fortunately, help was at hand. In the late Sixties, at the age of 28, Will took a decision that dramatically altered the direction of his life and the lives of many who knew him. He left behind the humdrum existence of a young working-class jack-the-lad in industrial London and reinvented himself as a genuine working-class intellectual, unknowingly joining a distinguished line of autodidacts going back centuries.

One September evening in 1968 Will walked into Tower Hamlets College, just off the Commercial Road. He was welcomed by a young Welsh firebrand by the name of David Nicholson who became Will's evening-class tutor for the next two years. Nicholson taught economics and politics at the college and liked nothing more than teaching mustard-keen adult students like Will. The Welshman was politically engaged and stood as a Parliamentary candidate for the old Liberal Party in Will's constituency of Chingford, where he was roundly beaten by that old Tory curmudgeon Norman Tebbit. Nicholson was an inspirational teacher who fired the imagination of his students. He had incredibly high expectations and pushed adults through examinations before they had time to realize what they were taking on – they almost always achieved top grades. Nicholson was full of surprises. The last time I saw him he was bashing out a blues song on a pub piano just around the corner from his college.

Will took to the ebullient Nicholson immediately and, importantly, the Welshman gained his trust. He made the journey from Chingford through Stratford and down the Mile End Road to Stepney every Wednesday night in term time for the next two years. During this time he remained at his job at British Oxygen, continued to coach in school holidays, and indulge in his local football activities. In his first year at college the hard-working Williams achieved good passes in O level English, Economics, and British Constitution. The following year he successfully completed an A level in Politics and Government. It was a tremendous achievement for someone who had left school with very few qualifications.

This is not a book about the theory of education. However, it is worth dwelling for a moment on how adults learn. How does someone like Will, at the age of 30, set out to study the subjects he was taking at evening classes? Similarly, how does an adult tutor go about teaching mature students like Will? One way to get at these questions is to think about Raymond Williams's ideas of the 'masses'. He argued that there are no 'masses', only ways of seeing people that way. In other words, refuse stereotypes and treat each student as an individual. Dave Nicholson, Will's evening-class tutor, saw his students as individuals and taught them as individuals, rather than simply teaching a set course through formal schemes of work. Nicholson also had his students' best interests at heart. He knew they needed to pass exams and in many ways his classes were crammers. But despite the restrictions of examinations, Nicholson managed to teach his students to think clearly, write well, and produce proper academic essays.

Back in the late Sixties, there were no essay-writing classes or sessions on study skills. Will's tutor gave him the confidence to make his own decisions in the belief that he could read and interpret complex material and write about it. Of course, he made mistakes. One of the most difficult things for adult learners to accept is judgement of their work. Sympathetic tutors will criticize in constructive ways, enabling the student to make further progress. Good adult tutors build on their students' enthusiasm for their subject and keenness to succeed. Nicholson encouraged his classes to trust their own ideas and he produced some of the best adult students to come out of east London.

Forty years ago, A level students didn't need to worry too much about theory or cultural context. It was not until Will progressed to higher education that he would have to deal with the paradigm shift in the arts and humanities that led to ideas about the democracy of reading, feminism, and anti-imperialism. All of these things would have challenged his entrenched view of the world. But he needn't have worried. Those evenings in the East End proved to Will he had a brain and the big question for him now was: what next? He thought about his options long and hard and discussed his future at length with Nicholson and his friends at Daneford School. Teacher training was a real possibility. His passion for sport remained strong and Nicholson suggested that Will apply to a PE college where he could pursue his coaching interests. There were two possibilities: Brunel in west London or Loughborough, which would mean leaving London and his beloved Spurs. But Will had been away from home for his National Service and decided on the prestigious Loughborough College, as it was known in its pre-university days.

Back in the early 1970s many universities were prepared to accept mature students without the three A levels required of school leavers. His admissions tutors at Loughborough were impressed by Will's coaching experience and his academic achievements at Tower Hamlets and overlooked the fact that he didn't have a strong sporting profile. They would also have been impressed with the Cockney lad's army and work background and, to Will's astonishment, Loughborough offered him a place on their two-year mature students' diploma. In fairness, they had probably never met anyone quite like the chirpy factory worker turned academic. With his Loughborough place secure, Will thanked Dave Nicholson and his mates at Daneford School, gave up his job at BOC, left his parents' home of 30 years, and moved from east London for a new life in the very different cultural landscape of the East Midlands. He took to it like a duck to water.

To invoke Raymond Williams again (it is difficult to ignore him when writing about adult learning), his metaphor of a 'border' to describe the separation between ordinary working-class life and the life of the academic continues to resonate. For Williams, whose father was a train driver from South Wales, crossing the 'border' was fraught with difficulties. The Professor of Drama at Cambridge University, with his international reputation and list of acclaimed texts and novels, found it difficult to move between the high table of Jesus College and the kitchen table of his parents' modest home in Pandy. Williams had a deep loyalty to his working-class roots and never betrayed them, despite his fame and reputation. But he never lost that feeling of unease he felt moving between these two distinct worlds – the elevated one of Cambridge cloisters and academic theory, and the real world of railway signal boxes, working men's clubs, and making ends meet.

Malcolm Williams had no such inhibitions and appeared to travel between his life at home and his new life with consummate ease and assurance. It says much about his character that he was able to achieve a transition that has troubled others following a similar path. That's not to say he didn't have moments of panic when he thought he 'just couldn't do this any more'. But these moments were increasingly rare. Will bought a small house in Loughborough, which he shared with fellow students to help pay his mortgage. His housemates, ten years younger than the mature Londoner, were to become a great source of support and encouragement. Here he was at the premier PE college in the country with only a very modest sports profile, unlike those around him – as his friend Steve Mitchell remembers:

> I always felt that ability in sports was secondary and personality was the essential characteristic for advancement; something Malc had in buckets. He had a fantastic background in teaching soccer and sports, which was a great advantage.

Figures 2 and 3. *Left*: A young Malcolm Williams (far right) with friends in his favourite pub. *Right*: Following a distinguished teaching career in his 60s, 'Will' reinvented himself as a respected jazz singer. (By kind permission of the Williams family.)

Among his best friends were the England rugby players Fran Cotton and Steve Smith. Later Olympic champion and world record-holder Seb Coe became a particularly close friend. With these people around him, sharing his house, it's no wonder Will settled quickly into his new academic environment. It helped his cause that he volunteered to coach the football club's 3rd team – which earned him the respect of the younger students, who quickly nicknamed the 30 year old 'Gramps'. His tutors at Loughborough respected Will's work ethic and keenness to learn. He initially opted for drama as a subsidiary course but quickly dropped it for social studies, where he was in his element. His seminar group was particularly lively and Will was able to draw on his knowledge and understanding of social issues, as Steve Mitchell recalls:

> The group of a dozen was an interesting mix with Malc leading a very vocal group of mature students. It was an eye opener to me: a very green 20 year old straight from 6th Form. There would be heated debates on life in the East End, social injustice, and the relationship between management and workers.

Although committed to his studies, Will retained his independent streak. When he missed a ten-day outdoor education trip in North Wales, his tutor was understandably annoyed. The Head of PE summoned Will to his office. The conversation went something like this:

> Head of PE: 'Tell me why I shouldn't send you on the next course – what experience do you have of outdoor education?'

> Will: 'How about spending two years under canvas in Malaya fighting off the communist threat up to my neck in muck and bullets.'

He never went on an outdoor education trip during all his time at Loughborough. Will's quick mind, capacity for hard work, and sheer affability led him to become a respected and well-liked figure on the Loughborough campus. He was a free spirit but a good team player – a winning combination. Having gained his confidence in an academic environment as soon as he could, he signed up for a full-blown degree programme. Throughout his time in the East Midlands Will returned home for the long summer break. Ever resourceful, he took a job as a tourist guide, showing Japanese holiday-makers around the sights of London. Typically, he made himself an expert on Hawskmoor churches and the East End of Jack the Ripper and the Kray Twins. Some of the stories he told his groups stretched the truth to the limit, but they adored him for his wry smile and his ready wit.

Will remained single all his life, preferring to retain his prized independence. At Loughborough he had none of the responsibilities that marriage and children bring, so money was never really a problem. He had some savings and his lodgers' rent covered his mortgage, while back in the Sixties and Seventies mature students received relatively generous local authority grants for full-time degree study. As tuition fees were also paid by the LEA, it was relatively easy for a single person of 30 to live comfortably for three years on a full-time degree course. He never smoked and, unlike many of his London mates, wasn't a great drinker. To save some money Will swapped his gleaming Ford Consul for a modest second-hand Mini – his old limo might have seemed a little incongruous around the academic groves of Loughborough College.

Will's halcyon student days had to end sometime. He was always going to return to the capital, but with his brand-new degree he wasn't going to look for work at the cork factory or British Oxygen. His first teaching job was at Edmonton College down the North Circular Road. He sold his place at Loughborough to Steve Mitchell and bought a newish house out in the leafy suburbs of Essex. Almost immediately he realized this was a mistake. He missed the buzz of London and his old 'manor' – he was a fish out of water in his new suburban surroundings. So he exchanged the dull conformity of Essex for a new home just a short walk from his parents' house and his local, the Prince Albert, where the weekend jazz nights were as good as anywhere in London. In a neat piece of symmetry, Will's new house was directly opposite the public library where he had spent long hours studying for his GCEs and A levels at Tower Hamlets College.

After a few years Will got the job of his dreams – Programme Manager of Sports & Arts at Hackney College, one of the biggest FE colleges in

Europe. He told an interesting tale about his Hackney job interview. Chair of the panel that day was Caroline Benn, wife of the great socialist MP Tony Benn. During the course of the interview, Mrs Benn asked Williams, if he were to be successful, what would be the first thing he would do in his new job? The panel, expecting some management speak about team leadership or curriculum planning, laughed when Will answered, 'I'd buy a new Mini so I can get to work more easily, Mrs Benn.'

Amused by his cheek, Mrs Benn informed the mature candidate a few minutes later, 'We'd like to offer you the job – you can go and buy your new Mini.'

Will loved his work at Hackney and rose to the challenge of leading a team of enthusiastic professionals. What kind of leader was he? His close colleagues, Chris Morris and Neil Bromley, saw their new boss, with his shell suits and flip-flops, as proudly eccentric and unconventional. They remember the 'Geezer', as they soon dubbed him, as 'fiercely intelligent and prepared to challenge injustice and intellectual inconsistency head-on whenever they arose'. Will was old school. He had no time for political correctness, preferring to trust his instincts and take people at face value. He wasn't interested in whether someone was black or white, male or female. Having genuine substance was more important. When dealing with staff he always asked the question, 'Can you do the job?' He had little time for management theory, although he did enrol on a Masters course at Nottingham University, which showed that despite landing one of the top jobs in his new profession, his passion for learning had not deserted him.

Will would have been conscious that he had a responsible public sector job serving his community – that would have been the most important thing for him. Of course, he had realized the dream of changing his life, but personal fulfilment, satisfying as it would have been for the one-time manual worker, came second to his new responsibilities to the people of Hackney. He wore his new-found success lightly. When I asked him about his new job, he answered with typical modesty, 'It's great mate, I can be in the Albert 15 minutes after leaving college.'

These trademark remarks appear flippant but were undoubtedly disingenuous. Will was head of department in a major London FE college at time when feminism was at its height, and race and disability were extremely sensitive issues in education. He would have had to cope with and find a way around complex staffing and trade union issues. They were unavoidable. Using phrases such as 'nanny state' and 'political correctness gone mad' wouldn't have cut much ice with a member of staff claiming discrimination. It is a tribute to Will's intelligence and political sense that he negotiated his way through this minefield of social tension while remaining largely unchanged.

Will's personal life changed along with his new-found status – how could it not? He left behind the local girls from Chingford and Walthamstow and began to form relationships with educated, independent women who, though attracted by his Cockney charm, would have no truck with any kind of sexism. To his credit he made the transition effortlessly – perhaps the Mini was rather more cool than his old Ford Consul. But Will never deserted his local pub, a wonderful old Victorian building later demolished and replaced by an underground car park. It was in the Prince Albert that Will acquired his taste for jazz music. When he finally retired after 25 years in education, he reignited his love for jazz in the most astonishing manner.

For someone like Will, simply listening to jazz was not enough. He wanted to be involved in some way – he wanted to be a jazz singer. There was only one way he knew how to achieve this unlikely ambition. He enrolled on adult courses at the City Lit and Hackney College and set about learning how to be a jazz singer at the ripe old age of 60. Once he gained some confidence he performed on open nights at jazz clubs around London. He worked hard on his singing and attended music summer schools in Glamorgan where he worked with the greats of British jazz such as Bobby Wellins and Peter Coe. Will was accepted by top musicians as a proper jazz singer and sang with them on a regular basis. Once again he had achieved his dream. It's difficult to say which was the greater achievement: turning himself from a sheet metal worker, with no qualifications or prospects, into head of department at one of the country's top FE colleges with a prized MPhil to his name, or becoming a critically accepted jazz singer at the age of 60. One of these considerable achievements would have been enough for most people, but not Malcolm Williams. Of course, Will had no family responsibilities to distract him, no need to worry like Cyril Connolly that, 'the pram at the foot of the stairs is the enemy of promise'. But even without family preoccupations, Will's ferocious determination bordered on the heroic.

Adult education had provided Malcolm Williams with the opportunity to change his life and he seized the chance to realize every ounce of his considerable potential. The funding environment of the Sixties and Seventies helped. Today it is more likely that he would enrol on a part-time Open University course or an evening programme at Birkbeck College to achieve his degree. It would have taken him longer and cost a great deal more and it is unlikely the experience would have changed his life quite so dramatically. Will's experience raises the usual questions about the purpose and value of adult learning. Does a person changing his or her life in this way help the economy? Does it foster greater citizenship or produce a better-informed society? Does it compensate for shoddy schooling? Although committed to social justice, for Will, the journey was one he just had to make. He wouldn't have spent hours dwelling on it – there just wasn't time.

Malcolm Williams died in May 2006 at the age of 68 after suffering a severe chest infection. His close friend and confidant Seb Coe was by his side when he died. Coe has admitted that it was Will who showed him the poverty and hardship in boroughs such as Newham and Tower Hamlets and how important sport could be in regenerating east London. It was a lesson Coe learned well. London's bid for the 2012 Olympic Games was predicated on what he observed on his trips around Hackney and Haringey with his great friend. In some ways the rebirth of Stratford in 2012 was a tribute to the passion and resolve of Malcolm Williams. Will had accomplished so much in his life and was loved and respected as he moved from one adventure to the next. He made a significant contribution to improving the lives of hundreds of people in Hackney where he worked and he left the world a far better place. Will was from a different generation from Jack Stevens and lived centuries after the poet John Clare. But he shared these two autodidacts' thirst for knowledge and understanding and was part of the same tradition. His friend Steve Mitchell spoke eloquently at Will's funeral and his words expressed in language he would have understood what everyone who knew him felt: 'Willy ... you were a very, very special geezer.'

A new world of opportunity

The autodidact tradition was largely male dominated. Jack Stevens's wife was bright and well read, but with seven children there would have been little time for anything other than her prodigious family. It would never have occurred to her to take up any kind of formal study. This would have been the situation of intelligent working-class women in the 1950s. But over the past 30 years the position of women in adult education has changed dramatically. The expansion of local authority and state-funded adult learning from the late 1960s has signalled the end of the autodidact tradition. Until very recently, every town and city in the UK boasted an adult education centre or community college. And of course there was always the WEA. The introduction of the Open University in 1971 provided the crowning glory. Most centres offered courses at entry level and the annual September enrolment was one of the highlights of the social calendar, with queues snaking along the streets or around playgrounds. Courses were cheap and subsidies generous. The obstacles to learning for working-class men and women had been removed. From the late 1960s, the women's liberation movement began to influence every aspect of our culture and education was at the forefront. Encouraged by sensitive course planning, women began to form the majority of adult learners – a key theme throughout these pages.

Gradually, women began to benefit from the new opportunities and to challenge the formerly male-dominated sector. One such woman was Tracy Selby, who bravely found her own way round the new model of adult education in the manner of the old autodidacts. Like many women, Tracy overcame prejudice, discrimination, and a debilitating illness in the course of her academic adventure. But she was never deterred as she threw herself into her studies. As Tracy moved successfully through the different levels, the end result was not what she expected.

'NOBODY IN AR FAMLY IS GOOIN TO UNI'

Brian, my stepfather, in his broad South Yorkshire accent, once told me, 'Nobody in ar famly is gooin to uni, tha working class and thal goo art n gerra job!' At the age of 16 I went on a youth training scheme (YTS) and did office skills and just worked and felt that I would never be inspired again to study. I managed to resit O levels and after that I studied for A level French at evening classes at my local college. Then I saw a law course with a September start. I had become interested in law and this was my opportunity. So I enrolled on the Higher Certificate in Paralegal Studies. I was pleased that the method of assessment was by written assignments and it was good not to have to be faced with exams at the end of the year. I laboured over that first assignment for weeks. We handed in the completed assignments for assessment. I had scored a distinction. I felt like there was no stopping me now.

At the end of term a lecturer came into college from Sheffield Hallam University to mark our files. At the end of the evening the lecturer and moderator told me that my work was above the standard needed. I was numb and stuck for words – 37 years of age and at last I had started to succeed. My stepfather's words all those years before echoed around my head, 'Tha working class, tha not gooin to uni!' I actually took my certificate for the Higher Certificate in Paralegal Studies just to show my family. 'Has tha seen Paddy, thar Tracy's got hersen a law qualification?!'

Next I decided to enrol on the Fellowship Award in Matrimonial and Family Law, which involved a research project. We attended tutorials once a term so I was concerned about distance learning – would this be all distance and little learning? How would I manage without a class every week and a tutor other than attending tutorials? I need not have worried because the tutor was there if needed. Before I could say 'distance learning' it was the end of another year and I had really become accustomed to this new approach. This might be a route for me in the future…

I gained a Distinction Specially Commended for the Fellowship Award and was pleased to read the assessor's comments: 'I am surprised to see that you do not work in law, your research is better than some that do!' I have treasured this assignment since 2005 and began to feel as though I had hit the jackpot! My background is in local government as a clerical officer, which I did for 20 years. It had been years since I had updated my administration skills so I decided to enrol for a Legal Secretaries Diploma with the Institute of Legal Secretaries and PAs, which was by distance learning.

I scored 100 per cent in the Tort Law module. At the end of the course I got my Legal Secretaries Diploma, and by this time my thoughts were heading towards a degree… I decided to update my word-processing skills via a distance learning secretarial college. Distance learning, I hear you think! Will there be an ongoing pattern here? I had enrolled at Level 2 but as I was doing so well the tutor upgraded my course to OCR Level 3.

I had an interest in health and I decided to try medical audio transcription and medical word processing. The distance learning malarkey was working well for me and showed me that anyone with determination and an interest can most definitely achieve something. By now my thoughts of degree study were very much embedded in my brain. Through 2008 I toyed with the idea of a law degree at Sheffield Hallam University but I did not want to spend up to eight hours per week in the evenings at lectures on the part-time study route. I also considered why I would need a law degree. I did not want to be a solicitor, so maybe advice studies at Stoke on Trent was an option – and it was distance learning. Then one of my work colleagues mentioned the Open University. Now if she could do it and manage a full-time job, then surely I could. I got the prospectus and discovered the OU did a BA Open Degree with or without Honours. After much pondering, I signed up for 'Starting With

Law' on the Openings programme. It was my first 10-point module but it felt good to be on the way to that BA Open Degree. I was sure that distance learning would be the best thing for me.

My tutor on the Openings course had suggested the 60-point 'Rules, Rights and Justice' law module at Level 1. The materials arrived for it and there were about nine text books and another two that were large, thick readers. New to me were university tutorials. I attended some of them in Sheffield and I enjoyed being there. Being part of a class felt good. The aspect that bothered me the most about degree study has been the essays and assignments. After nearly four years of being a student I still find writing essays a challenge. It is the fear of failing that worries me most. The essays were on themes such as compare and contrast and discuss. I had never done this before so needed to learn a whole set of new skills. But I passed the assignments and achieved the full module at the end of the year. Now I had 70 points at Level 1 – a good start. So what next?

I had been told during my annual performance and development review at work that my degree studies were 'pointless and irrelevant to my work as a clerical officer'. I was gutted and appalled that someone who was supposed to be a manager had such a negative view of education. But I did well and achieved the module. At that time my health was not so good. I had struggled at work and with my studies and I had a feeling that I would fail the final course assessment. I had just started a short course on DNA science and within a few weeks I was admitted to hospital with DVT, which went to multiple pulmonary emboli followed by major abdominal surgery for a serious health condition. Despite my ill health my determination to get the degree was stronger than ever. I did fail the module but enrolled for a resit. I was chuffed when I passed the second time; I had started to fight back. I had never failed an assessment in my Open University study but at least I know that although most students fail at some point, they generally bounce back.

Since my first module I have studied and successfully passed courses in Intermediate Spanish and Introduction to Counselling. I now feel that I listen more attentively and also value people's opinions more just by my listening to them. I have surprised myself because I always said that I would never have the skills to study social science.

The final module for my degree was really difficult. It was a critical evaluation of a journal article on counselling research. It was too scientific for me and we will have to see the results of this, but I think that I will at least pass, which is all that I need for the BA Open Degree without the Honours.

Moving forward then... I will pick up more modules from February 2014 with the Open University. I expect to study a language at Level 3 and a mental health module. In time I would love to do postgraduate study or even another degree, perhaps in modern language studies. My studies remain one of the most important personal goals for me and have been a great way of getting my life on balance again after illness and redundancy. If my degree studies eventually take me somewhere then that will be a bonus, I feel that given the right opportunity there are so many possibilities, and, at 46 years old, I am still a young woman.

Like Jack and Will, Tracy showed enormous determination and perseverance to achieve her academic objectives. Her path was often uncertain and sent her off in directions she would not have anticipated. A combination of IT skills, legal, social science, and language courses has taken her to a degree and possibly a Masters. Tracy navigated her way through a mix of local college, adult centre and Open University provision, a real test of her determination. Gaining in confidence, Tracy fought off prejudice, health problems, and her own fears to gain the degree she was desperate to achieve. Her story and the experience of many women like her provides a bridge between the historic male autodidact tradition and a more enabling, open, and extended model of adult learning that has transformed the lives of thousands of adults young and old. They are grateful beneficiaries of the expansion of opportunities in the sector that was denied to our pioneering autodidacts John Clare, John Pearman, John Burns, and those old soldiers, Jack Stevens and Malcolm Williams.

Chapter 3

A sign of things to come

The Mary Ward Centre: the friendly place to learn

Adult learning received a boost in the nineteenth century when several eminent Victorians reasoned that extending education to working-class adults would help to alleviate poverty and stimulate social change. Their thinking was that teaching the poorer sections of society to read and write would not only 'civilize' them but raise their skill and employability levels. Matthew Arnold, Andrew Carnegie, and John Passmore Edwards were all passionate advocates of adult education for social change and spoke out against the prevailing laissez-faire political philosophy of the day. These leading intellectual figures and benefactors raised some of the most important questions of the age. How far was the pursuit of wealth of benefit to ordinary people? How far was religion addressing issues of extreme poverty and inequality? What should politicians do to alleviate the conditions of the poor – economically, socially, and culturally? A better-educated working class was at the heart of their ideas on social change. This nineteenth-century philanthropy-driven strand of adult learning differed from the mutuality and fellowship of the improvement societies, the socialist guilds, and the early WEA. The charitable model lacked the political thrust of the latter, and although desperately keen to help the poor, the largely liberal-inclined philanthropists were far less interested in radical politics or waging class war.

There was at least one dissenting voice in the nineteenth century who believed that radical ideas, although important, would not in themselves bring about fundamental social change. Not content to express her disapproval of social injustice, Mary Ward was a woman of action and impatient for change. Her educational enterprises were a visible testimony to her indefatigable spirit and prodigious energy. Australian-born, Mary was the grand-daughter of Thomas Arnold, founder of Rugby School and niece of Matthew Arnold, Professor of Poetry at Oxford University. Ward was a Victorian novelist, author of the influential *Robert Elsemere* (1888), a three-volume work that provoked a national debate on the church's role in promoting social change. The eminent writer was at the centre of a group of prominent thinkers and educationalists that included her uncle, Matthew, and her brother-in-law, Leonard Huxley. The Arnold and Huxley families were important influences on British intellectual life and it was inevitable that a bright girl like Mary would be inspired by the intellectual excitement in which she grew up.

There is little doubt that the Ward household was a place of high seriousness and learning. The problem for Mary was that as a child, she was hardly around to experience the thrill of it all. Having been dispatched to far-flung residential schools of dubious quality when she was as young as 6, Mary was left to cope with childhood and the pressure of being a teenager alone. She had a truly miserable childhood. Her stern Victorian father, Thomas Arnold, and subservient mother hardly ever visited Mary while she was away at boarding school and their letters were few and far between. Her father, on the odd occasions when he did write to his eldest daughter, signed himself, with typical insensitivity, 'Yours, T. Arnold'.

There is little question that Mary was a difficult child, at times even out of control. Sending her away to fend for herself at such a young age was either meant to improve her challenging behaviour or simply to remove her from the family. There is little doubt it was the latter. Mary endured an unhappy childhood and her father's clear preference for the company of her brothers influenced her later desire to improve educational opportunities for working-class girls and young women. But there was another, more benign, influence on this clever young girl. In the darkest days of her dreadful schooling, one of her teachers stands out like a shining light. Anne Clough had a profound effect on Mary's life and the lives of generations of intelligent young women in the late nineteenth century. Ms Clough, who taught at Mary's first residential school in the Lake District, was a devout high Anglican who lavished praise and attention on bright young girls such as Mary. Educationally ahead of her time, she provided individual learning plans for every girl who showed promise. But:

> ... the greatest asset which Clough brought to the education of a girl like Mary was her lifelong conviction of the equal importance of education for girls.
>
> (Sutherland, 1991: 28)

Anne Clough dedicated her later life to promoting higher education for women. In 1871, exhausted by her years of schoolteaching, she took up the wardenship of a residential house on the edge of Cambridge and became an influential figure in the university. In 1879 Ms Clough's undoubted talents were recognized by the university when she was appointed the first principal of the women-only Newnham College, the very same year in which

Somerville Hall opened in Oxford, with her former pupil, Mary Ward, as the college's first secretary. As John Sutherland points out:

> Thus, the two careers which had crossed at a village primary school in 1858 recrossed two decades later in the opening of Oxbridge to the female sex.
>
> (ibid.: 129–30)

Despite the benign influence of Anne Clough, Mary could not forget the bitter memories of her early education. Moreover, she remained angry at how her intellectual development was neglected simply because she was a woman. She wrote:

> As far as intellectual training was concerned, my nine years from seven to seventeen were practically wasted. I learned nothing thoroughly or accurately.
>
> (quoted in Sutherland, 1991: 29)

Unlike her brothers, Mary understood she was being prepared by her parents for marriage, not a career. In 1865 this clever teenager at last found some happiness when she transferred to a boarding school in Bristol and enjoyed two years of the intellectual excitement and emotional support she was desperate for at home. Mary finally left school in 1867 and returned to the family home in Oxford where her father had taken up a lecturing post.

Throughout her childhood and teenage years, Mary was a compulsive writer and had produced a number of unpublished short stories when, to her delight, 'A Westmoreland Story' appeared in an edition of the *Churchman's Companion*. On her return to the family, Mary was, of course, expected to fully embrace her training in the running of the household, but the aspiring young writer had other ideas and set about developing her embryonic writing career with her usual passion and determination.

On 6 April 1872, Mary, not yet 21, married the journalist Humphry Ward. Her father was far from happy and later remarked to Mary's grandmother:

> Mary will have to look at her housekeeping very closely ... it is her duty to postpone literature and everything else to the paramount duty of keeping a straight and unindebted household.
>
> (ibid.: 40)

The couple settled in Oxford where Mary set about making herself familiar with French, German, Latin, and Greek, while developing a profound and lasting interest in the social and educational issues of the day. The couple had three children, but Mary was not content to play the conventional role of an acquiescent Victorian wife and mother. In her 20s she continued to write furiously, publishing magazine articles, children's stories, novels, and works of translation. Slowly her work began to attract attention and in 1903 her novel *Lady Rose's Daughter* was the best-selling novel in the United States, while *Robert Elsmere* was published in Britain to critical acclaim. The themes at the centre of most of Ward's work were the nature of Victorian values and the essence of Christianity. A recurring theme in her writing was that in the age of improvement the church was being left behind.

Robert Elsmere features a young Anglican priest who undergoes a spiritual crisis. At odds with his church he decides that if faith is to mean anything it should meet the needs of the poor and disadvantaged. In the novel, Elsmere establishes a settlement in the East End of London called the 'New Brotherhood' where he sets about putting his ideas into practice. The notion inspired much debate among the chattering classes of the day, which encouraged Mary to turn fiction into fact by launching her own centre along the lines of the successful Toynbee Hall in London's East End. It would be stretching a point to describe Mary as a socialist. However, there is no question she was passionate about social justice and believed that providing free educational opportunities to the working class would be the most effective way to achieve effective and long-lasting change. Turning away from her literary preoccupation with the failings of the established church, Mary now believed that education was where she could do the most good. She was about to put her reforming ideas into practice.

In 1891, at the height of her literary fame, Mary duly established a settlement at University Hall in Gordon Square, London – a tribute to her tremendous energy and social commitment. Both Oxford and Cambridge universities and Eton College had set up charitable settlements in the East End, as the ruling class finally accepted the extent of poverty in the inner cities. Mary, though, chose Bloomsbury in west London to put her ideas into practice, rather than the area of most need across the capital. But she knew Bloomsbury well and was aware of the pockets of poverty, prostitution, and deprivation a short walk away in notorious districts such as Euston and King's Cross. Unable to rid herself entirely of the pull of religion, the original purpose of University Hall was to provide, 'improved popular reading of the Bible and of the history of religion' and to secure for residents of the settlement, 'opportunities for religious and social work'. The twin aims of religious and social teaching soon proved incompatible as disagreements began to develop between residents who wanted more Bible reading, and others who argued that University Hall should play a more active role in the local community. Their differences were irreconcilable and within a short time a small group of socially minded residents led by Ward broke away and secured a new site for their activities in Marchmont Hall, east of Tavistock Square, where they could practise their good works unencumbered by religious distractions.

Marchmont Hall, situated close to the University of London, was an immediate success, much to the disappointment of the more religiously inclined residents of University Hall. Mary taught at the settlement herself and was encouraged by the sheer enthusiasm of her students. Many of the local adults who attended the centre simply wanted to learn to read and write or do some basic arithmetic. But Mary was particularly impressed by the more able students' willingness to tackle complex ideas. Buoyed by the success of Marchmont Hall, the energetic and resourceful Ward decided to seek funding for a new, purpose-built centre that could accommodate a more varied range of activities. Among those she wrote to was the great Victorian philanthropist and advocate for public libraries, John Passmore Edwards. Thanks to the energy and commitment of Passmore, along with Andrew Carnegie, the Public Libraries Act was passed in 1851 and the Cornishman seemed the ideal supporter for Mary's dream project. But to her immense disappointment, the great benefactor politely declined her initial request for funding. However, her persistence eventually paid off when Passmore at last agreed to support the new project. In a letter to Mary in March 1895, he agreed to pledge up to £7,000, increased to £10,000 if Mrs Ward agreed to name the new facility the 'Passmore Edwards Settlement'.

Passmore was not a distant sponsor but took a close interest in the project and advised Mary on contractual arrangements with the landlord of the proposed site, the Duke of Bedford. For her new initiative Mary chose a site a few hundred yards from Marchmont Hall, just off Tavistock Square. The new building in Tavistock Place was a short walk from the University of London's Senate House in the heart of leafy Bloomsbury. One of the reasons Mary wanted to leave Marchmont Hall was that it was too far removed from her target audience, the deprived neighbourhoods to the east of the relative affluence of gentle Bloomsbury. The new location was just a short walk from the squalor of King's Cross, Pentonville, and the streets leading off the City Road.

Following their brief to the letter, two young architects, Dunbar Smith and Cecil Brewer, who had been residents of the original settlement, won a competition for the design of the new centre. Their success was an astonishing achievement given that it was the partnership's first major project. The building was judged to be one of the finest Arts and Crafts designs in

London and an inspirational moment in British architecture. For some at the time, the building was much more than an inspired work of design. The *Architect's Journal* of 2 August 1889 believed that Tavistock Place was 'a social ideal being expressed in architecture'.

The fusion of social purpose and design would have delighted Mary. Opened in 1898, the new facility became the site of great intellectual argument and discussion. The historic debate on women's suffrage between Mary and Millicent Garrett Fawcett was held at the centre in February 1909, when the host was decisively defeated. Mary's opposition to women having the vote sits uneasily with her interest in social justice and equality – one of the ironic complexities of the time. She defined the purpose of the new centre as providing, 'education, social intercourse and debate of the wider sort, music, books, pictures, travel'.

Tavistock Place was a great success. It was a hive of activity and the projects were many and varied. In addition to the adult education programme, the centre housed the Invalid Children's School and a pioneering Vacation School, intended to occupy local children during the school holidays. Mary and her daughters also found time to support Coram's Fields, the nearby foundling hospital. Given the diversity of the centre's programme, which reached out to mothers and young children, people with learning disabilities, and adults from all backgrounds keen to learn a wide variety of subjects, the rather awkwardly named Passmore Edwards Settlement can be seen as a prototype community college, a century before their introduction by far-sighted local authorities such as Devon, Cambridgeshire, and Leicestershire.

Exhausted by overwork and increasing ill health, Mary Ward died in 1920, her life's work completed. The centre stands as a tribute to her. The building was renamed the Mary Ward Settlement in honour of its founder and in 1970 was given its current name, the Mary Ward Centre. The adult education programme continued to expand and in the latter part of the twentieth century became the main focus of the centre. Later provision of legal aid and financial advice to people on low incomes was added as the centre adapted to the shifting needs of the times. Mary's project not only survived, but grew and prospered to become one of the most exciting and vibrant adult education institutions in London, and to this day it has stayed true to the founder's principles and ideals.

In 1982, the trustees of the Mary Ward Centre negotiated with London County Council to relocate their activities to a more spacious building in nearby Queen Square. Having survived two world wars and four changes of address this venerable adult establishment was well prepared to face the fresh challenges of twenty-first-century London. The new home, a

Grade II-listed building, is light and airy and just a few yards from Russell Square and the sprawling campus of the University of London.

In 1992, after settling easily into its new home, the Mary Ward Centre was awarded Special Designated Institution by Act of Parliament status and later granted Beacon status in recognition of its exceptionally high standards in teaching and learning. Today the centre has a thriving outreach programme, a popular vegetarian café, and a recently acquired and refurbished building at 10 Great Turnstile in Holborn. A Legal Centre was opened in Boswell Street before the Second World War, providing legal aid and financial advice, and continues to form an integral part of the wider activities of this admirable organization. The centre's broad range of activities reflects the founder's passionate belief in social justice. Housing and welfare assistance, legal advice, and learning opportunities are all integral elements of a community service designed to support local residents in need of help and guidance. This is no ordinary adult education centre, important as those noble institutions are to our culture.

Mary Ward CBE lived an extraordinary life and her achievements were, by any standards, quite astonishing. An internationally respected novelist, Ward was one of the first women magistrates. She was well connected, numbering US President Theodore Roosevelt among her friends. As if that wasn't enough, this gifted and determined woman founded a pioneering centre of adult and community education that continues to prosper. Mary would be delighted with the way in which her brainchild has flourished. Spread over two sites, today the centre boasts art and sculpture studios, performances spaces, well-equipped classrooms, and excellent community facilities while continuing to pursue the original aims of the founder. Perhaps the most impressive feature of the modern Mary Ward Centre is the way in which the programme has been adapted to meet the needs of the capital's shifting population.

Principal Suzanna Jackson describes the programme for 2012–13 as: 'packed with a broad range of interesting and stimulating courses for everyone from beginners to experienced learners'. This modest statement may be true but it fails to tell the whole story. Health studies, computing, business management, and accounting sit alongside courses on dance, fitness, jazz, and yoga. The centre has developed innovative partnerships with the British Museum, Birkbeck College, and Kew Gardens and offers practical sessions on weaving, knitting, and design. An over-60s programme and adult literacy courses sit at the heart of an imaginative curriculum, along with more traditional academic subjects such as philosophy, psychology, and history – a very impressive programme by any standards.

Once solely funded by wealthy benefactors, today the centre has a mixed economy. Most of the funding comes from central government, although up to 50 per cent of the total student fees make up the remainder. The majority of the 5,000 students are between the ages of 35 and 55, while the second largest group are the over-60s – the eldest student at the centre in 2012 was 102 years old. Around 15 per cent of the centre's students are disabled and the Queen Square building has been adapted to fit the accessibility needs of users. A highly significant 22 per cent of the learners are from ethnic minorities, many from Eastern Europe and Africa. Several of Mary Ward's students are trafficked women – a tribute to the success of its outreach programme. An orchestra, choir, and theatre group further strengthen the sense of community within the institution and help to develop a strong college ethos and sense of identity. The centre has a retention rate of around 90 per cent – an indication of the excellence of its teaching and the relevance of the programme. One of the major reasons for this impressive figure is the personalized learning initiative that runs across departments and encourages achievement and progression. Clearly the students feel secure with their tutors, support staff, and the progress they are making. They are all extremely proud to be part of the Mary Ward experience.

One of the most impressive elements of the Mary Ward's programme is the range and quality of its outreach work. It is this partnership work that provides the greatest insight into the purpose of a modern adult education centre, one that differs from the founder's original vision. The Mary Ward Centre is 'a place for ideals, a place for enthusiasm', claims the centre's website. I saw the ideals and enthusiasm at first hand at the British Museum one early spring Sunday in 2014. 'My Viking Boat' was a creative arts exhibition held in the Museum's Great Court. Ten local, multi-ethnic community groups led by the Mary Ward outreach team came together over a period of 12 months to create a magnificent display of over 200 boats at the museum's prestigious Viking exhibition. Maddy Fisk, the head of outreach at Mary Ward, explained how the groups combined their resources in an impressive piece of co-operation. In partnership with Tasneem Khan, head of the British Museum's community team, Maddy led this ambitious project and the results were stunning. While visitors enjoyed the display, parents and children flocked to the creative workshops staffed by both professionals and volunteers. As successful as the day was, the process leading up to it was equally as important. A look behind the scene reveals the extent to which adult learning has changed over the past 20 years.

In addition to the museum and the Mary Ward Centre, the principal 'My Viking Boat' project partners were the Fitzrovia Neighbourhood Centre,

Chadswell Healthy Living Centre in King's Cross, and the Christopher Hatton Primary School in Camden. Maddy outlined what the partners hoped to achieve with the project:

> We aim to raise awareness and change lives. The project is about capacity building in the community.
>
> (Interview, March 2014)

This is a radical departure from the traditional aims of building-based adult learning. However, as the hundreds of visitors on the day would, I am sure, agree, the project was more than simply a community development scheme, of which there are many in Camden and elsewhere. The quality of the artefacts on display at the museum on that splendid Sunday are a visible confirmation that the project was definitely a learning initiative with a strong emphasis on creativity, as Maddy explained:

> Our outreach projects are mostly creative because visual education is more likely to work with our target groups than more conventional text-based learning.
>
> (Interview, March 2013)

This is a long way from the traditional adult education class and the Mary Ward staff should be commended on their innovative approach to adult learning in the inner city. It was clear from my discussion with both students and staff at the centre that their outreach provision is not student-led but driven by a dedicated staff team who have a deep understanding and empathy with their community. The decision to focus on creative activities is a good example. Students who have little or no English or who have literacy problems, or whose confidence has been drained by their life experience, are unlikely to enter the doors of a formal education centre; even if they did they could not possibly cope with text-based subjects.

The outreach students at Mary Ward are registered on courses in the same way as other adult students. First, this means the outreach work is fundable and at the same time the students feel they are on a legitimate adult programme. These 'courses' need to be extremely flexible in their delivery as students may be late, may need to leave the class early, and may be unused to the discipline required of regular attendance and good timekeeping. Many of the participants on the outreach programme lead chaotic lives and have to learn to cope with the demands of attending a structured course. An outreach yoga class provided by Maddy Fisk's team began chaotically with students arriving late, missing sessions altogether, or constantly taking calls on their mobile phones. Led by a sensitive and very patient tutor, the group gradually acquired the skills necessary to become successful members of a ten-week class. A further element of Mary Ward's effective community strategy is the tracking of students' progress, attendance, and changing personal circumstances. Given such a diverse catchment area, tracking has to be done extremely sensitively and with great care. With such high retention rates, the staff at Mary Ward are clearly well trained and their tracking strategy is a good indication of their flexible approach to course design and student behaviour.

One of the boats in the 'My Viking Boat' exhibition was a beautiful woven felt creation that stood proudly at the centre of the display. The boat was designed and made by Catrina, who lives just down the road from the British Museum. Catrina has been a catalyst for the project, supporting others, offering advice, and generally being an encouraging presence. She is also an active member of the Chadswell Healthy Living Centre and helps as a voluntary youth worker in the notoriously challenging King's Cross area. Angie is a friend of Catrina and was also an active member of the project. She became involved after she attended Chadswell hoping to talk to someone about her heavy smoking habit. Plucking up courage, Angie turned up one morning and to her surprise received a very warm welcome. With the help of specialist staff Angie was able to give up smoking within a few weeks. But she didn't stop there. Simply by picking up a leaflet and chatting to her new friends, including Catrina, Angie joined a French beginners' class at Mary Ward – she has since progressed to intermediate level. It is fair to say that Angie's life changed the day she walked into the Chadswell Healthy Living Centre.

Participants came to the 'My Viking Boat' project through very different routes: Catrina through her community work and Angie through her determination to quit smoking, but both through a local health centre. One of the entries that stood out that day at the British Museum was a glorious red and gold sailing ship created by Lisa, a young mother whose children attend the nearby Christopher Hatton Primary School. Lisa heard about the project from the school and soon became a key member. Surrounded by her family, she talked about her boat with tremendous pride and enthusiasm. Lisa found it difficult to comprehend that here she was at the world-famous British Museum with crowds of people from all over the world enjoying something she had made with her own hands.

Maddy and Tasneem and their colleagues worked extremely hard and effectively to make the project succeed. Without their dedicated professionalism and knowledge of their communities, not only would there have been no 'My Viking Boat' exhibition that Sunday but scores of local people would have been deprived of an experience that, for many of them, enriched, even changed their lives. Of course, there are hundreds of these kinds of project across the country, but few of such range and quality and involving so many people from such diverse backgrounds, cultures, and religions. The 'My Viking Boat' project was modern adult learning at its very best and would not have happened without the Mary Ward Centre's outreach programme. Working closely with other London boroughs and community groups, Mary Ward offers over 100 community-based courses. In addition to the 'My Viking Boat' project partners, the centre's partners include the Calthorpe Project and the Hopscotch Asian Women's Centre, to name just two. Their reach is deep and wide and one of the key factors in their success is that many of the activities are arts-based for reasons we mentioned earlier.

Others have used Mary Ward's creative approach to learning with equally impressive results. There is a school in Selma, Alabama, that was shut down in the early 1990s after the National Guard occupied the building following a series of corridor shootings. The school was situated in a poor, black neighbourhood on the edge of what Americans describe as a 'housing project'. The school was reopened two years after the shootings following the appointment of a specially selected headteacher, a charismatic Baptist pastor from the more affluent white area of the town. The school was redesignated a single-year establishment, acting as a bridge between primary and secondary school. I spent a few days at the school soon after it reopened and enjoyed the kind hospitality of the new head, Bill Simpson. One evening around midnight Bill drove me around the poorest areas of his district before we stopped for a welcome drink at the intriguingly named Jesse James Hotel, close to the bridge from where Martin Luther King led the great Civil Rights march of 1964.

Bill explained that from day one, with the support of the School District, the school introduced a creativity-based curriculum in the belief that this would motivate and inspire local youngsters. It was an extremely high-risk strategy, but the gamble paid off. Within a couple of years the school became a model for every poor, black neighbourhood in Alabama. At the heart of the school curriculum were two of the most innovative projects I have seen in over 30 years in education. Ballet dancing and a butterfly garden are among the last things you would expect to find in a school in a rundown community in the American South, but both were an enormous success and incredibly popular with the students. To see 12-year-old boys and girls from such a tough place clad in brightly coloured tutus and leaping around the school hall was a sight I will never forget. The butterfly garden in the school yard was set around a high wall decorated in beautiful artwork that the students painted and repainted every few weeks. The popularity of these two creative projects motivated the students to apply themselves in other, more traditional subjects. The local community began to trust the school and support the teachers. Children with poor reading and numeracy skills saw a reason to come to school. As a result, attendance improved dramatically. It would be wrong to think that the students watched butterfly behaviour all day clad in ballet gear. Literacy and numeracy were given a high priority in order to prepare the children for their next school. But creativity was at the heart of everything. As the head of maths told me, 'my department is here to serve the arts'.

Our new 'superhead' was no zero-tolerance, neo-disciplinarian, but a gentle, sensitive educator who cared about the students and their families (although it has to be said Bill was no pushover). But, like the Mary Ward outreach programme, the creative curriculum was at the heart of the school's success. And like the leaders of the London project, Bill Simpson had a deep understanding of his catchment area, planted strong community roots, and stayed to watch them grow. At Selma, for a few years at least, butterflies and ballet shoes replaced guns and bullets.

The London Borough of Camden is a better place for the work of professionals such as Maddy Fisk and Tasneem Khan. The outreach work at Mary Ward is a great success on a number of levels and is critical to the success of the centre's mission. But it represents only a minor, if important, part of the general programme. As Maddy has said, their work with the local Bangladeshi community and its disproportionate number of children under 5, the Bollywood dance classes, and all the other myriad partnership initiatives in Camden and beyond, is really more about community development and support than traditional adult learning. So we need to return to the Queen Square building for a look at the formal adult curriculum.

Back at the main building we find a more familiar setting for adult learning. From the Ofsted Report of 2009 we know that the centre has over 5,000 registered students of all ages and an ethnic profile of 28 per cent. Around 76 per cent are female and students are drawn from across the capital. The percentage of students claiming concessionary fees is 46 per cent, while those declaring a disability have risen to 15 per cent. I am sure Mary Ward would be shocked to discover that the Passmore Edwards Settlement she founded in 1898 was still going strong 116 years later. She would be even more shocked to learn that such a high percentage of today's students are women. As we discussed earlier, this dramatic gender shift has been the most significant development in adult learning over the past 30 years and is a trend repeated across the UK.

The Queen Square building is very welcoming, with a deserved reputation for being a 'friendly place to learn'. Students cover a broad range of subjects including languages, computing, business, health and social care, and a broad range of humanities and arts-based provision. In fact, something for everybody and a programme that would make the founder, if she could see the hustle and bustle of Queen Square today, a very proud lady indeed. What would also delight Mary Ward is that her centre achieved Outstanding in every category in its 2012–13 Ofsted inspection. But a few abstract statistics and a brief programme description tell us little about the beating heart of the Mary Ward Centre. I made several visits to Queen Square over the academic year of 2012–13. On every visit I received a warm welcome from Suzanna Jackson and marketing and communications assistant Imogen Petit. During the course of my visits I was very fortunate to meet a group of students who agreed to become participants in the research for this book. There isn't the space here to include each student's story, so I have selected two who perhaps best represent the essence of the Mary Ward experience.

Shanti has cerebral palsy and her life changed dramatically the day she walked into the Mary Ward Centre. Shanti writes with passion and depth of insight. This is her story:

Shanti's story

Hello my name is Shanti. My education has been challenging because I have moderate learning difficulties and because of this it has taken longer. My tutors showed me that it was possible to overcome a learning difficulty by working with it not against, and most of all not to give up.

My passions are photography, writing, music, and history. Photography is my favourite – it teaches me so much and one can never stop learning it. I have written two books unpublished and did it for fun. I wanted to be a writer for ages.

When I came to the Mary Ward Centre it was a brand-new start. I attended an adult literacy workshop to improve my spelling and grammar with one-to-one support. It was slow but it was great. I found I was getting somewhere. To go at my own pace was good and at the same time I was discovering how I was learning. My education has changed me as a person in so many ways, it is the chance to do my very best. I hated school, it was very disheartening and I thought I had no future.

In my first year at Mary Ward I did an art and design foundation course with my mother and it was great. I got so much support from the tutor and my mother, at the end of the course I got a merit. I have tried to overcome people who make me unsure of myself. They have been so many, but the Mary Ward Centre helped me and gave me a great opportunity to grow and be heard. This has changed me as a person and made me believe in myself more, it has made me stronger.

In my life in education I have found myself in very uncomfortable situations and the Mary Ward is no exception, but it has given me the space that I need to find my strength to serve and learn. The education at the Mary Ward Centre is great and I have been listened to. I have had problems with other students but this has only made me stronger to stand firm on my own two feet.

Often it feels like my disabilities are not there and it's great. The more I find out about how it works the more I am able to get around it and hopefully overcome it. But one has to be passionate and know a lot about it before one can really work with it in the correct way. From all my education I see myself teaching photography and working in an office doing the best I can and hopefully making it on my own. Being at the Mary Ward has given me hope.

There is something about silence that makes me think more clearly about the thing that I am studying and I have found it becomes easier to get the work done and it makes it more achievable. Taking a real break from study can make a real difference, but I have always found the enjoyment of study magic!

Currently, I do yoga because I have cerebral palsy and it is much better than physio. My learning difficulties seem like a huge block that always comes out of the blue. It is how one deals with it that can be the key to making it. It is a pain and one does get frustrated but the more one can find out about it the more one can do and the farther one can go. From being at the Mary Ward Centre one huge thing that I have learned is that there are no limits and if they are there, always they can be worked on.

Shanti is an exceptional young woman. Her thoughts on stereotyping, how schools and FE colleges failed to meet her needs, her ideas about silence, and the way she has used visual images to help her study are all powerful insights into the life of a young person determined to find her own way in the world. It was at the Mary Ward Centre that she finally found the encouragement and the support she required. Shanti is now at the heart of the centre, attending classes, helping fellow students, and working in the centre's busy reception.

Mother of two Annalisa Cacorgiani is currently studying for an Open University degree but began her studies at Mary Ward. Annalisa was very keen for others to hear about her educational journey. Here is a short extract from her story:

DESIGN IS MY PASSION

I'm Annalisa, I'm 49 years old, Italian. I moved to London due to my husband's job at the end of 2008 with two children who are 6 and 8 years old now. I didn't study English before so when I arrived I knew maybe the most common ten words. After one week in London I started an evening English language course. I did all the ESOL Cambridge exams, from Entry 1 to Level 2. In 2009 I started to attend courses at Mary Ward Centre, in design, Photoshop beginner and advanced, Illustrator, Publisher, writing for TV, communication at work, English pronunciation. I used to bring my little son Rocco to the Mary Ward Centre, and while I was attending classes I left him in the crèche that was in the basement.

I built up my CV and I started to look for a job – it was long, unsuccessful. I was so discouraged that last year I eventually decided to apply for a degree course at the Open University: design and Innovation BA/BSc Hons business pathway. It's a 360-credits course. In February 2014 I completed the first 90 credits. Design has been always my passion. I felt different, motivated. I started to work from home, as an online moderator. Studying and working from home turned out to be the better solution, considering that my family has been always my priority.

Going back to university has deeply impacted on my family's daily life. I have monthly deadlines so my free time gets tight especially close to the exams. I'm so concerned at not being able to prepare the assignment on time that I became extremely self-disciplined and organized. My approach towards study has drastically changed since my old times at school: it's something I do for myself, my project, it's a journey towards my final goal of working in a field I'm passionate about.

It's a long journey and I've met many people in my situation, coming from different backgrounds, many of us going back to university after more than 20 years. We all struggle to memorize concepts, to write essays or reports in the requested academic way.

People around me ask me why I decided to go back to university; my answer is why not? It's like seeing another horizon, opening my mind. Fitting job and university around my family life is crazy but strangely I've never been as confident as now.

Annalisa's story is one of great determination and courage. Finding herself in a new country with a young family, she learned a new language, settled her young children into a new culture and set about trying to find work. As if this wasn't enough, Annalisa was determined to find a way of nurturing her own intellectual and creative instincts. She found what she needed at the Mary Ward Centre and later the Open University. Mary Ward would have been thrilled to see Annalisa cycling through the busy London traffic loaded up with books and papers on her way to college for a class or examination. Annalisa is unwavering in her single-mindedness, but she is not unusual and is one of thousands who, despite all the obstacles that stand in their way, are determined to follow their dream.

Figure 4: The Mary Ward Centre overlooking Queen Square in the heart of London's Bloomsbury.

The stories of Shanti, Annalisa, and the participants of the 'My Viking Boat' project illustrate the kind of opportunities the Mary Ward Centre provides for its students. In the summer of 2014 a festival of the arts, 'This Woman's Work', was held at the Queen Square building. The festival was designed to foster participation in the arts by women of different ethnic, cultural, religious, and social backgrounds. Funded by the Royal Female School of

Art, the festival was a terrific success and an illustration that Mrs Ward's ideals forged back in the 1880s are in very safe hands. The centre is a shining example of what is best in adult education and is a beacon of light in one of the most diverse areas in London. In the words of Raymond Williams, Mary Ward offers local people the resources 'for a journey of hope'. But Williams knew more than most that specialist adult colleges such as Mary Ward remain vulnerable in the face of political reaction.

A journey to understanding: the Working Men's College

> It always upset me that my dad never learned English and that my mum could not read or write in any language at all. I always thought that it really damaged their life chances. My dad was a great carpenter. He made everything and anything you could imagine, but he just could not get a job in this country that fully used his skills because of his lack of English. I always felt that was really wrong.
>
> (Satnam Gill: interview for
> *Black History Monthly*, 26 October 2012)

The Working Men's College (WMC) is one of four specially designated colleges in London and one of the oldest adult education institutions in Europe. Like the Mary Ward Centre, the WMC draws its students mainly from the London Borough of Camden. The borough has a complex and transient population, with desolate housing estates a few hundred yards from trendy loft apartments and expensive Georgian terraces. Camden is also undereducated. Less than 50 per cent of the population have a degree and school leaver attainment is lower than the national average. The wards surrounding the college have high levels of multiple deprivation and nearly a third of local residents are members of minority ethnic communities, many of whom have English as their second language. Camden has been a working-class borough for centuries, but this is changing and the old and familiar political and social language is no longer adequate to describe the population of this complex place.

Adult learning has long been at the centre of attempts to improve community life in Camden. The WMC was established in St Pancras in 1854 and is the oldest adult education institution in the UK. The college was founded by an unlikely group of nineteenth-century Chartists and Christian Socialists in a time of serious social unrest. College Founder J.M. Ludlow wrote:

> In the whole course of my life in this country I never recollect such a period of unrest and alarm as in March and the first ten days of April 1848.
>
> (Notes of a talk at St Margaret's House, December 1894)

Following revolutions in Europe in the late 1840s, rioting occurred in towns and cities across the UK, led by Chartist leaders demanding radical political reform. On 10 April 1848, over 150,000 Chartists and fellow travellers descended on Kennington Common in south London. The demonstration remained peaceful, with 100,000 police mobilized should the protestors decide to cross the river. Several of the founders of the WMC witnessed the dramatic scenes at first hand. It would take many years before all of the Chartists' demands were met, long after their leaders had left the political stage. But Chartism's influence struck deep into the heart of British political and cultural life. The ideals of the movement were particularly influential in the early years of adult education. In his history of the WMC, Harrison wrote:

> There is a need for all educational history to be directly related
> to its social context; but especially is this so for adult education.
>
> (Harrison, 1954: 1)

Harrison's contention that education and politics are inextricably linked is an unfashionable view – few adult learners at the WMC or at Mary Ward Centre today would admit that they see themselves as part of a political movement or social revolution. But in the mid-nineteenth century there is little doubt, as we saw in Chapter 1, that adult education was part of a more general social movement for change. The years between 1848 and 1854 saw the formation of the WMC and the arrival of the college's first students and, as Harrison suggested, 'it is in the ideals and social turmoil of that period that the origins of the College are to be found' (ibid.: 14). There is little doubt that the founders of the WMC were directly influenced by the events at Kennington Common. Frederick Maurice (the first principal), Richard Litchfield, John Ludlow, and Thomas Hughes – author of *Tom Brown's Schooldays* – were all Chartist sympathizers. A great supporter in the early days of the WMC was the author of the children's classic *The Water Babies*. An intensely religious man, Charles Kingsley attended the Kennington protest and was troubled by what he saw. A few days later he declared, 'I am a Church of England clergyman. And I am a Chartist.'

This diverse group of churchmen, secularists, friends of Chartism, and Christian Socialists were the energy and inspiration for the Working Men's College. The founders' initial challenge was to forge genuine links with the working-class people they were so keen to champion. They met as a group at Frederick Maurice's Bloomsbury house following the Kennington demonstration to discuss how they might establish contact with local activists. The winter of 1847–8 had been particularly grim for working people with soaring bread prices and high unemployment – a toxic combination.

Protest was at its height and the authorities feared the worst. But the WMC founders speculated that Britain, despite the profound inequalities and social discontent, remained the richest industrial nation in the world and that things would improve. There could be no better time for the group to introduce their idea for the WMC.

WORKING MEN'S COLLEGE

THE OLD HOME IN GREAT ORMOND STREET

Figure 5: The old Working Men's College building in Great Ormond Street. (By kind permission of WMC.)

Several of the men who became founders of the college had previously established 'missionary' work in the Bloomsbury area of Camden. In 1848 they introduced a night school in Little Ormond Street where they provided instruction in the three Rs to poorly educated local workers. The initiative was a partial success and ran on the principle carried over later into the WMC: all teachers should provide their services free of charge – a revolutionary idea even in the nineteenth century. For most of the staff it was their first brush with any form of poverty and illiteracy, but despite their good intentions the night school lacked a coherent programme and any direct contact with organized local groups.

A blend of Christianity and socialism, combined with a passion for reform, was the underlying political and philosophical principle that stirred the founders of the WMC. With the decline of Chartism, their radicalism found an outlet in the working men's associations, the British equivalent of the Paris *ouvrières*. The idea of associationism, as it became known, was, according to Harrison, simple:

> ... they were to be associations of working craftsmen carrying out their production on a co-operative basis. The capital was to come, ideally, from the associates themselves, but ... the wealthier Christian Socialists were prepared to advance the capital on loan.
>
> (ibid.: 1)

Strongly opposed to laissez-faire economics, Christian Socialists, frustrated at the failure of Chartism, turned to the co-operative movement as a more practical way of achieving their aims. The turning away from a broad political movement in the mid-nineteenth century in favour of a more fragmented political dissent did not dampen the enthusiasm for social change for the founders of the WMC. Instead, in a moment of inspiration, men such as Maurice, Hughes, and college secretary Jennings began to believe that working-class education would provide a more lasting means of achieving their radical aims. As the revolutionary zeal of the late 1840s began to give way to a more familiar British pragmatism, the founders of the WMC saw their opportunity. It was a crucial moment in the history of adult education. Reflecting on the opening of the WMC in 1854, Hughes wrote to Jennings:

> ... the squabbles and idlings and swindlings and incompetence of the workmen in the London Association ... convinced Mr Maurice that they had to be educated before they would be capable of the self-restraint, staunchness and obedience which are absolutely necessary.
>
> (ibid.: 15)

Hughes and his colleague knew that without the support of the working class there could be no radical social change. His somewhat patronizing tone masks a genuine concern about the economic condition of working people and the need for things to change. But without the necessary skills, the organized working-class movement floundered. Maurice and the other founders 'recognized the need of the working classes for education ... to fit themselves for this higher type of organization'. Convinced of the way forward, the founders settled on their own organizational principle, as Maurice explained, 'A college expressed to my mind ... precisely the work we could undertake, and ought to undertake, as professional men.'

The Working Men's College in London was established directly to assist the process of social change and as part of a wider political drive towards social justice. The college historian J.F.C. Harrison, himself an adult tutor, described the experience of a typical WMC student of the nineteenth century:

> In joining the Working Men's College, an artisan was ... doing more than just getting a bit of schooling, or passing a quiet hour innocently. He was, in effect, making a quiet but effective protest against the society in which he found himself. His social philosophy and his ideals were proclaimed.
>
> (ibid.: xviii)

Harrison's words resonate down the years. If we forgive the gender bias, his statement helps to explain the motives of many adult learners in the twenty-first century. But the new principal and his board wanted more than a facility that provided a hastily organized programme of classes for local artisans. They wanted something more: a spiritual entity that fully expressed their ideals and those of their students. The wanted a proper, full-blown college based on mutuality and fellowship. The opening of the WMC in 1854 was a momentous moment in the living tradition of British adult education as it entered an exciting new phase. The old Mechanics' Institutes were being replaced by a more collegiate approach to teaching, learning, and curriculum development led by the WMC in Camden.

Ground-breaking as the WMC initiative was at the time, the college doors remained open exclusively to men. In 1874 Maurice and Francis Martin did set up the Working Women's College, later renamed the Francis Martin College. But the sister college ran into financial difficulties through poor organization and lack of support, before being absorbed into the main college in the 1960s. The Francis Martin College finally closed in 1967 – the year the WMC decided to allow women students through its doors. We have seen that one of the most significant trends in adult education of the twenty-first century is the dramatic increase in the number of women students. But at the time of the opening of the WMC this encouraging development remained stubbornly 150 years away.

The idea of a purpose-built college had both philosophical and practical roots. By the end of the nineteenth century an expansion in student numbers created an urgent need for more space and improved facilities. The college staff and board of directors began to think about a planned curriculum that required specialized accommodation and equipment. Common rooms, a well-stocked library, a main hall, and canteen facilities were all essential features of a college based on the Oxbridge model. Science labs, art studios, a theatre, and sports facilities were all urgently needed to enrich the student experience. As in an Oxbridge college, the common room became the spiritual heart of the WMC. It was used for a whole variety of private and public uses, including lectures, public debates, and as a meeting place for local community groups. One of the WMC's most important functions every year was the Furnivall Supper, established by founder F.J. Furnivall. Every Christmas, right up to the 1980s, a Christmas meal was provided by the college for local senior citizens.

With the addition of a museum, a delightful theatre space, and the Maurice Hall, the founders had achieved their ambition to establish an educational facility for local adults on the model of an Oxbridge college. The Working Men's College, built on the principles of fellowship and association, was fit and ready for the new educational challenges of the twentieth century. To this end the building was extended in 1936, funded partly by the College Endowment Fund. A second common room was added and playing fields were acquired at Canon's Park in Edgware. Crucially, and in the spirit of the times, two new laboratories were added, replacing the College's outdated science facilities. The WMC now offered a broad curriculum ranging from the arts and theatre studies to the core subjects of science, maths, language, and literature. It was an impressive offer. Close to the hearts and minds of the founders was a commitment to a liberal education defined by Sir Wilfred Griffin Eady, WMC principal from 1949 to 1955, as:

> Something you can enjoy for its own sake, something which is a personal possession and an inward enrichment, and something which teaches a sense of values.
>
> (ibid.: 191)

Part of the management tradition of a liberal education, as set out by Sir Wilfred, was that teachers should give their time voluntarily and that both staff and students should be known as Members of College, invoking the spirit of fellowship and equality that were central tenets of Chartism and Christian Socialism. Any change in these laudable values would threaten not only the philosophy of the founders, but also the very financial future of the WMC.

Pressure on these sacred values increased in modern times, as students began to demand more certificated courses to improve their employability. Gradually, the college started to introduce certificated programmes that required more specialized teaching. By the end of the 1970s the ideologically driven system of voluntary tutoring appeared anachronistic and a threat to the future of the WMC as other London colleges began to modernize their curriculum and staffing arrangements. The College Council finally bowed to the inevitable and in the early 1980s the voluntary tradition was abandoned. For over 150 years the college had maintained itself through donations and the income from investments. This happy state of affairs could not continue indefinitely. The decision to pay staff led to an immediate drain on the college's reserves to the point that the future of the WMC itself was at risk. The only recourse was to join the rest of the sector by seeking aid from local authorities and central government. The public paymasters inevitably wanted more transparent governance and management structures that, some argued passionately, ran counter to the college's founding principles. The modernizers took the reasonable view that new structures and systems were needed to cope with enhanced levels of financial and educational accountability.

The modernizers triumphed and the WMC is now a full member of the national adult learning network, but at the cost of losing its nineteenth-century values of providing a liberal education based on the principles of fellowship and mutuality. Those values were compromised when the college turned to the government for its core funding. Or were they? As Richard Hoggart (1995) reminded us, this remains one of the key questions in any investigation into the aims and objectives of adult learning in the twenty-first century, and a central issue at the heart of this book. Has the march of vocationalism and a results-based culture compromised the ideal of adult education rooted in the Industrial Revolution? Hoggart argued that by funding vocational courses at the expense of more traditional liberal learning, successive governments have neatly sidestepped the issue of adult learning for social justice. The old traditionalist makes a strong point. But the truth is that the sector would have disappeared long ago if it had not adapted to change – that has been one of its greatest strengths.

As the WMC evolved, the college moved from Red Lion Square to Great Ormond Street before settling in its current home in Crowndale Road in the heart of Camden Town, a few miles from affluent Bloomsbury and a recently gentrified King's Cross. The new facility was opened in 1904 by Sir William Anson with the foundation stone laid by the Prince of Wales, soon to become George V. The building was Grade II listed in 1964 and has undergone considerable improvement and expansion through the years. Today the original name of the Working Men's College sits proudly, if somewhat ironically, over the portals of the impressive and welcoming front entrance. Set in the busy heart of Camden, the college is unrecognizable from the modest building that opened its doors in 1904. The imposing new entrance sits proudly at the centre of a thriving, multi-ethnic community as diverse as anywhere in Europe. Walk up the steps and into the glass-fronted reception and you are quickly greeted by well-trained and friendly staff. The atmosphere is calm, with students and staff moving purposefully to and from their classes. That the WMC is one of the best of its kind in the UK is without question as this notice on the college website proclaims:

> In March 2013 WMC was proud to become the first London College to achieve Outstanding under the new Common Inspection Framework. Both Visual Arts and ESOL were graded as outstanding together with Teaching, Learning and Assessment, Outcomes for Learners and Leadership and Management.
>
> (www.wmcollege.ac.uk, accessed February 2014)

Congratulations all round. But the WMC did not always have such a glowing reputation. The notice continues:

> We have been able to commission a research report tracking our journey from failing and broke in the late 1990s to outstanding and thriving in the 21st century. Our researcher aims to identify the effective initiatives and lessons learned in the process which we hope may be useful to other Colleges and Adult and Community Learning Providers.

What brought about the change? Current Principal Satnam Gill explains:

> This Outstanding grade from Ofsted is a real tribute to the amazing work being done at WMC by our hardworking learners and teachers. On leaving, the Lead Inspector said, 'This is what

adult education should be.' It is wonderful that during a period of considerable financial problems for adult education, Ofsted has recognized that WMC is a fantastic place to study, that we deliver outstanding results for our learners and the local community, and that many of our learners have been enabled to progress to further study or into work.

Figure 6: The greatly extended new WMC building in Crowndale Road, Camden, at the heart of one of the most multi-ethnic areas of London. (With special thanks to photographer Angela Inglis.)

Gill has led the remarkable turnaround in the fortunes of the WMC largely by gaining the confidence of his staff, the local community, and the students. As the Ofsted report says, 'This is what adult education should be' (Ofsted Report on the WMC, 2013).

So, no more concerns about adult learning raising political consciousness or acting as a hotbed of revolution that terrified both conservatives and liberals around the Ruskin Strike of 1909. The truth is, places like the WMC and the Mary Ward Centre, operating in front-line areas such as Camden, are simply responding to the constant demographic change and transformation of the inner city. Social fragmentation has blown apart the comforting certainties about rigid class divisions on which political values such as socialism emerged and could be nurtured through adult education. People such as Raphael Samuel at Ruskin and Raymond Williams at the WEA promoted the socialist philosophy of adult learning and built their careers on their beliefs. Modern adult educationalists like Satnam Gill have a more pragmatic approach to their work that, despite its lack of a clear political perspective, has a deep attachment to social justice. Their instincts are collaborative and the WMC is as likely to work in partnership with services such as housing, welfare, health, and employment as they are with trade unions or political parties. Gill and his colleagues are responding creatively to the innumerable needs of their communities, mostly in the context of diminishing resources.

Today's adult educators have a very different concept of social justice from the distinguished pioneers of adult learning. Perhaps this is less exhilarating than the heady days when politically aware students were sold the idea that education was the road to revolution, but it is arguably more effective. The modern approach has greater flexibility and is rooted in political realities. Social justice in the inner city is no longer about the liberation of the working class and the victory of socialism, but more about helping individuals to improve their job prospects or enhance their careers, providing opportunities for creative expression, and assisting individuals and community groups to alleviate the effects of poverty and discrimination. More specifically, one of the most important and urgent aspects of their work involves teaching those for whom English is not their first language. The vocabulary of social justice has changed from working-class solidarity, socialism, or old-style revolution to include terms such as 'inclusivity', 'disadvantage', 'access', 'diversity', 'discrimination', 'minority', and 'gender issues'.

The WMC is in the vanguard for this new model of adult learning. With a total of 62 full-time staff, over 4,000 part-time adult students, and 450 community learners, the WMC is an important element of cultural life in this part of London. In 2013–14, 3,000 students followed courses at Level 1 or below, 575 at Level 2, and just 25 at Level 3. Women, unemployed people, and migrants formed the majority of students. These figures are an indication of the priorities of the college as it responds to the most urgent needs of its community. These statistics represent a clear vision and purpose and are a positive response to pressures from the local community and, importantly, shifts in national funding criteria.

In 2013, the WMC published 'Working Men's College: Our Journey to Understanding 1996–2013'. Funded by the Learning and Skills Improvement Service (LSIS), the report is the story of the college's route to success from near closure in 1995. The report should act as a manual of how to run a successful adult learning centre in an inner-city area. At the heart of the achievement of Satnam Gill's team, governors, and students is a clear strategic plan with challenging, but achievable targets. A further element of the plan was a change in perception of the teaching staff towards their students – a real shift in pedagogical thinking with echoes of Paulo Freire. Teaching staff have a new respect for their students and all departments across the college have high expectations, confident they are supported by a strong and effective management team. The plan is backed by impressive data gathering, detailed curriculum planning, a focus on equality and diversity, a clear departmental structure, effective staff development, and, crucially, a strong student voice. With a successful community engagement strategy involving over 50 partners and 25 ESOL (English for Speakers of Other Languages) venues, and clear progression routes for students, it is little wonder that punctuality and retention at WMC have improved dramatically.

In 1999 Lewisham College Principal Ruth Silver was appointed by the Learning Skills Council to lead the restructuring of the WMC. Silver had led Lewisham College to Grade 1 status and enjoyed a national reputation in further education. Her first action was to appoint Satnam Gill as principal. In 2001, Silver, now retired, was appointed chair of governors and the 'journey to outstanding' began in earnest. In addition to the restructuring referred to above, Silver, Gill, and their new senior team introduced a radical approach to teaching and learning to support their revised philosophical respect for their students. The new approach was guided by two principles: the need to achieve high retention rates at a time of funding restrictions and a focus on establishing clear and achievable progression routes for students. First, all staff accepted the need for a systematic programme of peer lesson observation. As the report states, there was, 'greater rigour in lesson observations supported by external paired observation'.

This resulted in:

> ... managers' increased ability to independently make grading decisions and to monitor teachers' action plans for improvement; improved use of ILT to enhance teaching, learning, assessment and self-directed study between sessions.
>
> (Ofsted Report, 2013)

Secondly, every tutor accepted the need to speak less in class in order to increase student engagement in the lesson:

> Teachers spoke less in class and more often took a monitoring role in very well-planned lessons, encouraging learners to use peer checking and support.
>
> (ibid.)

In addition to allowing students more time to interact with each other in class, volunteers were introduced to provide additional support. Staff and students at the WMC speak 15 languages between them and because of the multi-ethnic mix of students, tutors are aware of the need to build differentiation into more stimulating, topic-based lessons. With greater tracking of students, digital registers, and improved initial assessment it has become easier for tutors and departments to check progress. This detailed, but sensitive, approach resulted in an Outstanding Ofsted grade for teaching and learning. This philosophy rests easily alongside notions of fellowship and mutuality dear to the hearts of the founders.

A major building programme helped the WMC to offer its students improved teaching spaces, equipment, and IT infrastructure. In the spirit of respect, two prayer rooms have been introduced and there are excellent cafés serving food for every taste. One department that benefited most from the building project was art and design. Access to Higher Education courses were introduced in art and design, fashion, and music, while a Foundation Degree in Professional Practice in Art was validated jointly with Middlesex University in 2012. With clear progression routes in non-text-based subjects, the art department has grown from strength to strength. Practitioners from different art forms are invited to lead sessions as part of an attempt to add a vocational element to a creative subject.

In late 2013 I was fortunate to meet a group of 20 WMC students studying a range of subjects at all levels and for widely different reasons. The group was extremely diverse and included a young refugee from Somalia, two sisters who fled from persecution in Iran, two young Colombians who came to London to make a new life, and a woman with bipolar affective disorder who had taken successive courses over a ten-year period to build her delicate confidence. Ten of the group, all women, were studying childcare and wanted to work with children in a caring environment. Twelve of the group were studying ESOL courses. Interestingly, six women named their husband as the person who had most encouraged them to attend the WMC.

We have seen how the creative arts inspired students at the Mary Ward Centre and, if anything, the arts at the WMC have an even more central role in achieving the college's mission. One of the students who has benefited most from the reinvention of the arts at the WMC is Rosh Keegan. Rosh was one of a group who was willing to contribute her story and to have it included within these pages. Her story provides us with an insight into the student experience in the college's art department.

A SPACE TO GROW

Forbidden by my father to take art as an A level topic in my teens, this led me to suppress much of my love for the subject. As an adult I returned to it with much enthusiasm, studying interior design for four years. My career, however, swung from property finding and fund-raising to cooking – strangely I never developed a career in art, not until now that is.

Eleven years ago the sudden and untimely death of my 14-year-old daughter, Anastasia, tore my world apart. After some gentle encouragement from my sister, I began a simple and undemanding weekly ceramics course at a local adult education institute in Holmes Road, Kentish Town.

To be in the depths of art again was a huge comfort. I learned the basics of ceramics and enjoyed the process of learning again albeit finding it challenging. Slowly with care and compassion from the adults around me I began to weave back that which had unravelled within me.

A safe and guiding environment enabled me to explore my ideas and feelings through the medium of clay, mother earth, the most natural of elements. To this day I believe it was what saved me; it allowed me space to grow, to believe in myself as an individual; to express that which I could not in any other way. And now my journey has led me to become a practising artist ... I still attend classes at the Working Men's College – I won't ever stop. It's so enriching to be in an environment made up of adults from all walks of life. Where else could I find that?

In the last five years I have developed my individual style in ceramic sculpture. I have exhibited at various London art fairs and sold to clients around the world. I have had a winning piece displayed at the V&A. To make a living from my artwork is what I am heading for. My time at the WMC is invaluable; the support I gain cannot be matched. I love to work in this engaging positive environment and I love to be learning all the time.

Figure 7: In 2011 WMC student Rosh Keegan won the Theatre and Performance Prize at the V&A, and in 2014 she was shortlisted for the ArtGemini Prize, which promotes international contemporary art. Inspired by Picasso and aspects of primitive art, Rosh's work has sold in London and New York.

As a youngster, a stern father refused Rosh the opportunity to follow her passion. Years later, studying art at the WMC helped her to cope with a dreadful personal tragedy. Rosh flourished in the college's safe and secure environment and now she is building a successful career as a professional ceramicist. It is a heartening tale showing tremendous fortitude. The fact that Rosh is now a well-established artist in her own right but continues to attend the college – 'I won't ever stop' – is an endorsement of the work of the department and the college more generally.

Unlike Rosh, Dilwara (Dee) Taluker is not an art student but arrived at the WMC to study childcare. Dee is now a tutor at the college.

> YOU WON'T KNOW IF YOU DON'T TRY
>
> I came to the Working Men's College for the first time in 2011 to study childcare level 2. I left school at the age of 16 and started my family of four children. I had never gone to college but was adamant I wanted to pursue my education further.
>
> I heard about the Working Men's College while volunteering at my children's primary school, where I helped the parents who couldn't speak good English. It was then I got the opportunity to liaise with the college's outreach worker, who encouraged me to enrol. I have not looked back since. Shortly after starting the course I was asked to represent the college students by becoming a student rep.

Towards the end of my childcare course I was approached by the vocational manager and asked if I could temporarily facilitate and support the childcare class because of tutor absence. This gave me great confidence, with the knowledge that my hard work was recognized. I was then offered a wonderful opportunity to take a temporary job offer as an outreach worker. At first I wasn't sure, but my family and friends gave me nothing but encouragement and new hope, saying, 'Mummy you won't know if you don't try.'

Today I am a working mum all because the Working Men's College has opened a new door for me and has given me hope that I can work, learn, and be a mum at the same time.

Dee came through the college's outreach route and like Rosh warmed to the positive, life-enhancing ethos at the WMC. Dee is now a key figure at the WMC, acting as a bridge between staff and students and as an example to others of just what is possible. The college has worked extremely hard to provide a setting in which adult students are valued and respected and feel secure. Free from worries about exposure, humiliation, or failure, the students, especially those with a learning disability, are confident in their ability to succeed. Hazel Stephenson is dyslexic and with great courage offered to write about her time at the WMC:

FROM TWO TO 2,000 WORDS

Hello, my name is Hazel Stephenson and I am 49 years old. When I was young I hated school. So I left as soon as I could with no qualifications. I did not know what do, as it would always take me back to a moment in my life which haunts me. When I was 14 in my English class I had to read from a book called *Of Mice and Men*. I had to stand up to read. I started reading and after the third or fourth word I stopped because I could not read the next word in the sentence. I tried saying the word to myself, but I simply couldn't, so I stood there turning red with embarrassment, while the class started sniggering at me. I felt upset and stupid at not being able to read the word and I could not prevent the tears running down my face. I ran out of the classroom to the toilet. In the next class I sat and tried to do the work I had to do. This was hard because I did not understand it even after the teacher told me what to do. I also found it hard to do my homework.

I started working at a hairdressers from 16 until I was 18 years old. I worked as a caterer for quite a while, and during that time I started learning how to read. After I left the catering job I went on to become a childminder, which I loved doing. I also had my own children and I would read to them. If I did not practise reading I don't think I would have been able to do it with them. Then it came time for my older daughter to go to nursery. I would take her every day with my young daughter.

That's how it started. I would go every week with my little one, she would play and I would help to do cooking or craft work with the other children. It just went on like this for a while. Then after about two months the teacher came and asked me if I would like a job – I said yes. I started in June 1994.

They sent me to teacher training, which I would have to go to by myself. I would feel very unhappy because I would be there all day and they would want me to contribute to the subject. I could not because I would not always understand most of the time. I then had to start working in the reception class two days a week. I would have to do writing with some of the children in the class. I would panic and want to head for the door so that I could hide until it was time to go home.

Then about two years ago I decided that I had been at my job for too long. I felt that I wanted to have the qualification that meant that I was a qualified teacher assistant. So I went to my head to see if he would let me go to college. He said yes so I went to the Working Men's College to do a teacher assistant course. But before I could do anything I had to sit an exam. I went into a panic, but I sat down and did the exam. It was very hard because I did not understand most of the questions.

So I just keep going and I got to the end with great relief, then I waited for the teacher to check that I had got it right. I sat there shaking. I prayed I had got it right. When she came she sat down and looked at the paper. She said that I had failed. I was so upset that I wanted to cry. But while the teacher was going over the exam paper she said that she thought that I needed to do English and that I was dyslexic. All I did was nod my head because I knew if I said one word I would cry.

When I got home my family was waiting for me to see if I had passed the exam but all I did was to burst into tears and cry. After I had calmed down I told them what the teacher had said about the English and that I was dyslexic. So I decided that I would go to college and enrol in the English class. On the day the class started I was so nervous I did not know what it was going to be like. The second week we started reading. We would all have a turn to read out loud. It was really strange when it got to me, I thought I would be in a panic but everyone was having the same problem.

For the first time I liked going to college to learn. I also forgot about being dyslexic because I felt that I was doing OK. I would do my work in class and also do my homework with just a little bit of a problem. It was only when we got into our fourth term that I started to feel exposed. So I then went and spoke to my English teacher about the dyslexic problem and he said that he would sort it out for me. Then about two weeks later I got a call from Jackie asking me to come in about one hour before I stared college so we could do a test. She asked me a question and got me to write a few sentences. Once she had gone over the paper she said that I would need to have the test. A week later we did the test – it made me feel very upset because I just felt stupid that I could not do some of the questions, it made me cry again.

The lady that did the test was very understanding and we got though the test. I got through by the skin of my teeth. At the beginning of the next term I went to see the head of support and told her my problem. I was then going to start seeing a dyslexia teacher called Cheri and a support teacher in my English class after college. He was called Mohammed. After about two weeks I started to get better in the class.

So every time me and Cheri meet we start working on my problem, showing me that I could do it and that I was not stupid, though every time I would panic and want to hide. When I think about the way things are I never thought that I would be able to do the things I do now like travel away for a weekend by myself and stand up in the class and read.

In overcoming her fears and anxieties, Hazel showed immense courage and perseverance. It is an extraordinary tale. Her tutors at the WMC were patient and ceaselessly encouraging, recognizing Hazel's determination to overcome her disability and build a career. Hazel's experience at the WMC is living proof of the college's desire to support students through their programme. The college offers diagnostic assessment and dyslexia support that puts most schools to shame. According to The Dyslexia Association, schools have done little to help children with the condition, lack any expertise in the area, and in general have turned their back on the problem. An enquiry to the Dyslexia Association in December 2013 brought the following email response:

> Judging by the calls and emails we receive, dyslexia support in schools has been deteriorating in recent years, partly due to budget cuts. However, one of the main problems is that most teachers have had no training in understanding and supporting dyslexia, and many bright pupils who go on to university are not identified and supported at school. It is estimated that around half of dyslexia students at university were only identified while they were at university.

Tracy Elba-Porter has had to cope with homelessness, serious illness, the responsibilities of being a young single parent, and a chaotic lifestyle. Tracy's studies at the WMC have provided her with a route she has negotiated with great courage and resolve. The last time I spoke to Tracy she was a little depressed, but is gaining in confidence as she decides on her next step. It helps that she is seeing her estranged daughter and grandchildren on a regular basis. She knows her depression will pass and soon she will be able to concentrate on applying her new, hard-won skills and knowledge in a way that will move her life forward. Tracy's story is a tribute to the WMC, to Tracy herself, and to adult learning in general. One of the many virtues of adult education providers such as the WMC and the Mary Ward Centre is that they work extremely hard to help students like Rosh, Hazel, Tracy and, as you will read below, Wilfredo to cope with tragedy, illness and disability.

We have seen that the gender balance of students at the WMC and Mary Ward is heavily weighted in favour of women, but many male students have interesting stories to tell. One such is the WMC's Wilfredo Garcia-Sarria.

WILFREDO'S STORY

My name is Wilfredo Garcia-Sarria. I am a 43-year-old student nurse and I decided to restart my education after a 12-year gap. One of my beliefs is that education is a key element in building societies. I always say that if I got paid just for learning and studying I would have been a student for my whole life. I basically started my diploma in nursing when I thought my English was good enough to understand and communicate with others.

I felt like I needed to do something different, a bit more challenging. Another important motivation that triggered my desire to go ahead was and still is the fact that I like to engage with people from different backgrounds and cultures. Moreover, I think I need to be a part of and understand the system in which I live. I strongly believe that higher education is an excellent opportunity to help me reach all these objectives.

Every day I have a clearer understanding of what nursing is about and especially what it should be. One of my hopes is to have a very clear knowledge and understanding of the necessary skills that are required to be a competent nurse. Apart from skills that I have learned during these three years, such as diseases, anatomy and physiology, medication, and its function within the body, as well as the different types of treatment for every single condition, I have learned how to communicate with people. I have also learned that we have to see our patients as individuals in a holistic manner – in other words, looking into all different aspects that surround our service users, not just the diseases that affect them.

Definitely school works for me. There are two main aspects that are necessary for anyone to succeed in most careers and they are theory and practice; they go together. I think places like the Working Men's College provide the knowledge that teachers learn and help us to analyse how things work in a theoretical way.

Returning to learning after a long time gap has not been easy. However, when you look at who you were and who you are now, you realize the benefit of it. Education puts us on a different level, which means better understanding, better salary, new skills, and especially more chances to meet very interesting people that contribute immensely to the improvement of society.

The WMC attracts students from all backgrounds, languages, and cultures. Many have complex educational needs and some speak very little English. Over the past 15 years the college has worked hard to cater for all students and the student support service achieved an Outstanding grade in the 2013 Ofsted inspection. The current Conservative coalition government is threatening to 'modernize' the Disability Support Allowance (DSA) that has enabled colleges to provide financial and technical support for students with special needs. If the DSA is withdrawn or significantly reduced, the result will be catastrophic for Hazel and hundreds of other adult learners across the country.

The experience of our students at the WMC appears to question the traditionalists' view that adult education in the UK has been corrupted by successive governments' obsession with certification. Today, certificates and preparation for work are what many adult students want more than anything else. Of course, some continue to study for sheer pleasure and personal fulfilment, but in the new model of adult learning, political consciousness and social change are way down the list of priorities for today's students. The idea of education as a route to political understanding is not something most students think about. They are more likely to study to improve their job prospects or to seek a better life. This doesn't mean that adult education has lost its radical edge. Adult centres continue to be driven by a commitment to social justice and the alleviation of poverty and discrimination in all its forms. Almost under the radar, adult education has retained its integrity as an agent for social change in the way it helps students to develop and flourish, particularly in inner-city areas such as Camden. Despite politically driven attempts in recent years to destroy adult learning, the good work started in the nineteenth century continues to make progress. The longevity of the sector is a tribute to the compassion and professionalism of all concerned.

A successful restructuring programme that included new buildings, a redesigned curriculum, new department arrangements, and improved teaching and learning, together with a substantial outreach programme, were all key elements in the recent success of the WMC. Special events are a feature of the remodelled college. In recent years, the WMC has staged an International Women's Day and a World Aids Day, and each term guest lecturers are invited to enrich a particular area of the curriculum. There are also fashion and music days that generate a sense of anticipation and excitement. Everyone at the WMC should be congratulated on reinventing adult learning in an extremely diverse and disadvantaged area of London. The people of Camden have an adult learning centre of which they can be extremely proud. We now turn away from hectic inner-city London life and head north to the ancient university town of Oxford where we experience a very different kind of adult learning.

Chapter 4

Proud to be a Ransacker

Ruskin College sits contentedly in a leafy suburb just a few miles from the ancient colleges of the University of Oxford. Anyone visiting Ruskin for the first time would be impressed with the facilities, the seriousness and industry of its students, and, above all, the sense of stillness that hangs over the place. But we should not be fooled by the academic tranquillity. Behind the peaceful façade we discover historical tensions and controversies of such bitterness it is surprising the college has survived to celebrate its centenary year. Even a cursory glance at Ruskin's history reveals a catalogue of bitter disputes both within the walls of the splendid Great Headington campus and much more widely in the outside world.

The origins and tempestuous history of this noble institution take us to the heart of the central debates and arguments that have characterized British adult education for over a century. Ruskin College was founded in 1899 by two young Americans, Charles A. Beard and Walter Vrooman, specifically to provide educational opportunities for working-class men who were, like Hardy's Jude Fawley, denied access to a university education. Why did these two young idealists choose the city of Oxford in which to realize their visionary ambitions? Both Beard and Vrooman studied in the city, which, they believed, illustrated the acute social and educational divisions embedded deep in British society. However, the city's universities stood for the high academic standards they cherished, so where better to set up a college for the workers than Oxford?

For the next 100 years Ruskin College became a symbol of workers' education in its many forms and a voice for socialist thinking. Its board invited Mahatma Gandhi to speak at Ruskin during his visit to the UK in 1931 and the college was delighted when the inspirational Indian visionary accepted the invitation. In 1976 Labour Prime Minister James Callaghan gave his speech at Ruskin on the purpose and future of British education, and Tony Blair used the occasion of the twentieth anniversary of that seminal speech to deliver a keynote address on the eve of the 1997 General Election.

Figure 8: The original home of Ruskin College in Walton Street at the very centre of Oxford University. (By kind permission of Ruskin College.)

The history of Ruskin College is well documented and it is not my intention to offer a blow-by-blow account of its troubled past, but rather to set the context in which today's Ruskin students go about their quiet contemplation. Historically, Ruskin has always claimed a degree of uniqueness among Britain's adult colleges, on the grounds of its residential character and its original aim of providing a political education for aspiring leaders of the organized working class. One of my purposes here is to assess the college's claims for uniqueness. Established towards the end of the nineteenth century, Ruskin was not the first adult education centre in the UK, an honour that falls to the Working Men's College in London. But the Camden institution has enjoyed a relatively untroubled history compared to the conflict, brooding resentment, and rancorous debate that its Oxford cousin has experienced over the past 100 years.

At the time of the college's inception, Britain's role as the supreme industrial power was being challenged by technically more advanced countries such as Japan, Germany, and the United States. This came as a shock to British employers, who suddenly realized their policy of maintaining a cheap and uneducated labour force was short-sighted, not to mention exploitative. A more literate and numerate workforce was needed if British industry was to keep up with its brutally efficient challengers. In this early argument for adult learning, workers' education was linked to economic performance. This was not what the founders of Ruskin College had in mind at all. Ruskin was established to 'educate working men in order to achieve social change' – not to help industrialists maximize their profits. Beard, Vrooman, and their friends cared little for the priorities of wealthy capitalists. The founders' vision was based on educating workers for social and political change, but even this honourable and enduring aim carried within it a fundamental contradiction that, on at least two occasions in its 100-year history, threatened to bring Ruskin to its knees.

Fred Inglis, in his biography of that great thinker and cultural historian Richard Hoggart, writes:

> All historians of working class education are beset by the blood-stained dispute as to whether the WEA and the extra-mural department were politically radicalising or socially anaesthetic.
>
> (Inglis, 2014: 104)

Let's deal with the 'dispute' problem head on. That Ruskin has had a long association with the University of Oxford has proved a mixed blessing. Like all Oxford undergraduates, Ruskin students are residential and have access to the libraries and lectures of the wider university. For 100 years, Ruskin occupied a building in the heart of the university, close to the Georgian grandeur of Worcester College. From its very inception the link with Oxford was a decisive influence on teaching and learning at Ruskin. The college's relationship with the ancient university gave Ruskin academic credibility, but, some argued, at the cost of compromising its fundamental social and political values. This tension came to a head in 1909 when a student revolt, supported by the principal, Denis Hird, exposed the divisions in the most public manner. The action was motivated by a report on adult education, 'Oxford and Working Class Education', compiled jointly by Ruskin College, Oxford University, and the Workers' Educational Association (WEA). The report recommended closer academic links with the university and a more liberal academic curriculum. Following Hird's harsh dismissal for speaking out in support of the action, the students boycotted lectures and staged a defiant protest. The strike of 1909 lasted just two weeks but threatened not only the links with the university but the very existence of Ruskin itself.

What did the students want? And why did the principal risk his career to support them? The answers to these two critical questions expose the continuing rift between those who wanted a radical socialist college and others who favoured a less partisan approach, a more liberal curriculum, and a traditional pedagogy. The latter group sought greater academic links with Oxford University, which the students and their principal strongly opposed. The more liberal staff believed they should be teaching students in the interests of objective knowledge and social harmony, delivering a curriculum informed by 'the best that has been thought and said'. Hird and the striking students dismissed such pandering to academic interests as political treachery and argued that workers' education should focus on Tawney's 'really useful knowledge' and promote radical political action. The bitter row between the two opposed groups re-emerged 100 years later when two of its most celebrated staff publicly aired their opposing views on the future of Ruskin College on a national stage.

In truth, Oxford University didn't quite know what to do with the troublesome upstart. Steeped in history and tradition, the university exuded authority bordering on arrogance. As the poet W.H. Auden observed in his deeply evocative poem, 'Oxford':

> By the tower the river still runs to the sea and will run,
> And the stones in that tower are utterly
> Satisfied still with their weight.

The passionate, often vicious conflict between the two groups has bedevilled Ruskin College for over a century and centres on a clash of educational philosophies. The opposing sides in this ill-fated quarrel each have clear ideas about what the aims of education should be, what should be taught, and how. The position of the students and the newly formed Plebs League was quite clear. They wanted to teach a curriculum that exposed the injustices and inequalities in society. The aim, in this largely Marxist view of education, was to reveal the true nature of society to students, in the hope that they would return to their trade unions and workplaces and fight for change. Tutors designed radical courses on socialist economics and Marxist political theory and devised a student-centred teaching style decades before Paulo Freire's liberation model. In the early days Ruskin was part-funded by the trade unions, so it wasn't unreasonable for them to expect a say in the affairs of the college, including curriculum issues. The unions believed, quite reasonably, in words taken from Shelley, 'we are the many, they are the few'.

The opposition – authors of the 1909 report, governors of the college, the WEA (who were represented on the report committee), and Oxford University – had a very different, more traditional view of the purpose of adult learning. First, they argued for closer links with the university with regard to curriculum, teaching methods, and assessment. The traditionalists – we might call them liberals – regretted class divisions in society but believed that Ruskin students should receive the same education as any

Oxford undergraduate. In this way they would acquire the liberal social values enshrined in a classical university education.

This non-partisan, liberal philosophy of education won the day. The militant Plebs League had no faith in the report, fought hard against its recommendations, but lost the battle, if not the war. The governors appointed a new principal and when the dust settled life at Ruskin returned to its familiar customs and habits. The very idea of a separate working-class education began to fade as neo-liberal, 'radical chic' ideas offered a more attractive political alternative to the 'pipe and slippers' socialism of the old Left. But the echoes of the 1909 strike resonated loudly down the years, to resurface in the 1980s with a public ruckus that threatened the future of the college and the careers of some of its most distinguished staff.

The traditionalists might have emerged as victorious from the bitter dispute following publication of the 1909 Report, but it would be wrong to think that settled the matter. Ruskin continued to offer a programme of courses for generations of Labour-supporting trade unionists, most famously, John Prescott, Jack Ashley, and Dennis Skinner, who all went on from Ruskin to become Labour MPs and, in the case of Prescott, an influential Cabinet member. Prescott, who went on to gain a degree at Hull University, once said that entry qualifications for Ruskin 'were not GCSEs or A levels but your involvement in strikes'. Perhaps as a result of these eccentric entry qualifications, Ruskin continued to attracted world-class scholars and teachers such as Peter Wilmott, Hilda Kean, and Jane Thompson. But it was their two most celebrated academics who, in the 1980s, became embroiled in a fierce public row that raised the spectre of 1909 and exposed the ideological rift that the college had successfully managed to quieten for the best part of 70 years. That two of the UK's most prominent intellectuals were happy to air their differences in the most public way is an indication of how high feelings were running at this time.

Raphael Samuel and David Selbourne were public intellectuals in the manner of Edward Thompson and Raymond Williams. Both were successful authors with an influence extending far beyond the quiet anonymity of Auden's 'ancient stones' of the old university. Samuel, founder member of the British New Left, and Selbourne, idiosyncratic political thinker, both ruffled the feathers of Ruskin orthodoxy as they struggled to respond to a shifting political terrain. To overly simplify the nature of their disagreement, Samuel, the radical socialist historian, revived the spirit of the student strike of 1909, while the bristly neo-liberal Selbourne stood resolutely in the opposite camp. But it would be wrong to characterize the conflict as one between political extremes: it was as much about educational philosophy as political ideology, as we shall see.

Samuel, the people's historian and student champion, ran up against a formidable opponent. Erstwhile playwright, political philosopher, and prolific writer, Selbourne increasingly turned to journalism to express his views as his opponent began to win over Ruskin's staff and students. In an article in *The Times*, Selbourne set out his position and in doing so ignited an angry row previously confined within the college walls. To use one of Rupert Murdoch's newspapers to express his dissident views was guaranteed to turn up the heat and ensure the conflict had maximum exposure. Selbourne's central premise was that the Left had seriously misjudged the political mood of the moment, refusing to recognize what he termed as 'inconvenient truths' about the shifting hopes and aspirations of the British working class. The ideological gloves were well and truly off.

In his piece in *The Times*, Selbourne attacked what he described as the corruption of Labour politicians in the city of Liverpool. That seemed like heresy to those on the Left who saw Selbourne as, if not a fellow traveller, at least someone who could be relied upon to speak out resolutely against all kinds of social injustice. But Selbourne had crossed a line. He had betrayed Ruskin's very soul. If the attack on Liverpool Labour councillors wasn't bad enough, Selbourne's claim that class loyalties had been rendered obsolete by the 1980s further inflamed his dispute with Samuel who, he claimed, was 'romantic and illusory' in his obsession with a fixed and static class structure.

Such treachery was bound to antagonize those around the *New Left Review* group – who included Tariq Ali, Terry Eagleton, Francis Mulhearn, and Samuel himself. Arguably Ruskin's star academic, Selbourne couldn't have chosen a more provocative time in which to go public. With the Left licking its wounds following the trauma of the 1984 Miners' Strike and the brutal attack on the print unions by Eddie Shah and Rupert Murdoch, Selbourne timed his tirade to perfection. The miners were battered into submission at Orgreave and the print workers were next in line. Angry scenes at Grunwick and at News International's glitzy new headquarters at Wapping (of all places) spilled over into violence, with the police protecting the employers with every riot shield and baton charge they could muster.

Into this inflammatory industrial and political moment stepped David Selbourne, all intellectual guns blazing. Warming to his theme as self-appointed nemesis of the Left, the Ruskin historian accused Samuel of failing to recognize what the working class really wanted. With his not-so-subtle distinction between proletariat and plebeian, Selbourne argued that a crisis in class politics had begun to destabilize all previous certainties about class allegiance and working-class culture. For Selbourne, the working class were desperate to escape the means of production, not control them. Work was dirty and demeaning, not noble and dignified as the intellectual Left maintained. Workers were more interested in owning their own homes, flying off to sunny Spain during the factory shutdown, and spending their Saturdays rambling around shopping malls than they were about the minutiae of Marxist ideology. Selbourne accused Samuel of failing to engage with the realities of working-class life.

Of course, this public denunciation of one of the most distinguished and committed academics in the college's history went down like a political lead balloon back at Ruskin, the proud defender of working-class radicalism. Samuel's response was swift and unequivocal. The poster boy of left-wing intellectuals countered accusations of romanticism and nostalgia, describing the miners and printworkers as 'majestic heroes' who were at least prepared to stand and fight against the vengeful attack on working people led by press barons Eddie Shah and Rupert Murdoch, and Prime Minister Margaret Thatcher. Warming to his task, Samuel accused his Ruskin colleague of hitching a ride on the right-wing 'zeitgeist' of the British political culture of the 1980s. For Samuel, Selbourne's treacherous post-radical politics were a passing fad and nothing more than philosophical opportunism of the worst kind.

If the Selbourne and Samuel controversy echoed the Ruskin dispute of 1909, this time the victors were not those who wanted Ruskin to provide a liberal education to working-class adults by offering the 'best that has been thought and said', but a group led by Samuel, staunch keeper of the revolutionary flame. In the progressive era that followed the 1960s, the great historian's radical, student-centred teaching method was not confined to his own discipline. Teachers, researchers, and academics in a range of disciplines in the state sector turned away from the outmoded knowledge-led, teacher-dominated approach to education that had failed generations of working-class young people. In his book on Richard Hoggart, Fred Inglis, who cut his adult learning teeth at the WEA, explains the radical role of the adult tutor at this time:

> What he (Richard Hoggart) and his now famous colleagues in adult education – Shaw, Thompson and company – brought to their classes and powerfully deepened and extended as they taught them, was the certainty that intellectual discovery was a joint activity, that if knowledge was a product, it was more like a communal work of art than a facticity, that it was the precious end of joint study.
>
> (Inglis, 2014: 104)

This vigorous challenge to what counts as knowledge and Samuel's courageous attempts to demystify academic language began to turn the educational tide on an arrogant, but enduring epistemology. The outcome of the dispute was emphatic. Within a few months Selbourne had left Ruskin under a storm of protest and counter-protest. The poisoned atmosphere in Oxford at the time of the sacking of Denis Hird in 1909 was mild in comparison. Selbourne subsequently won his High Court case for wrongful dismissal against the college, but the fact that a highly respected historian with an international reputation could be allowed to leave Ruskin following a rancorous public dispute with a colleague was nothing short of sensational.

The problem for Selbourne was that Raphael Samuel was untouchable at Ruskin, largely because he enjoyed the unwavering support of colleagues and students. A former Communist Party member, Samuel left the party, like many others, after the Soviet invasion of Hungary in 1956. He had been tutored at Oxford by Marxist historian Christopher Hill and was steeped in British leftism. There is no question that he was the equal of Dorothy Thompson, E.P. Thompson, Eric Hobsbawn, and John Saville, the leading socialist historians of the day. An exceptional and popular teacher, Samuel's intellectual energy was legendary. He founded the *History Workshop Journal* in 1976 and was the inspiration for the influential 'history from below' method that, among other things, encouraged generations of enthusiasts to delve deep into the history of their own families. For Samuel, history should be a collaborative enterprise within which teachers, researchers, and students enjoy an equal relationship. Selbourne, the stubborn traditionalist, believed history should be taught as a body of knowledge (where have we heard this before?) and that students should be assessed in their knowledge of the subject in the time-honoured way.

In contrast, the aims of Samuel's philosophy of teaching and learning were built around students gaining intellectual confidence and acquiring research skills. This method – if you like, the 'student-centred' approach to teaching and learning – continues to come under fire from the political Right, who believe progressive education is responsible for most of the world's ills, including the drug culture, teenage pregnancy, gun and knife crime, obesity, and so on. Samuel sympathizer Richard Hoggart expressed his anger at the crude instrumentalism of a political Establishment bent on revenge as the Left's philosophy of education, shaped by Raphael Samuel and others, fades into memory:

> As I write, the latest Tory government is doing its best to wreck this lovely complex, delicate but sinewy fabric – by its characteristic insistence that any adult educational provision from which public funds are allocated should have a clearly defined vocational purpose; the rest is belittlingly, 'recreational'.
>
> (Hoggart, 1995: 161)

The Tory backlash against 'student-centred' learning and the relativism of multicultural education has shifted the terms of debate away from liberal and Left thinking. For now, the Right, with its price-tag mentality, is in control, much to the satisfaction of David Selbourne, we can assume. Samuel, with an enhanced reputation through his momentary victory at Ruskin, later moved to the University of East London, although he did retain a research and teaching role at Ruskin. Raphael Samuel died after a long illness in 1996. His progressive approach was valued highly by students, whose memories of school were often bitter and best forgotten. One of his more celebrated ex-students, the former Labour Deputy Prime Minister John Prescott, spoke for hundreds of Samuel's past students:

> Raphael Samuel opened my mind when I was a student in the 1960s. Until I went to Ruskin and met him, my education had come from correspondence courses, which I used to complete in a 14-bunk cabin after 20 hours' duty as a seaman on a liner.
>
> He had this tremendous understanding of the inner inferiority that mature students have in a society that tells them they've missed out. There wasn't an ounce of superiority in him. In those tutorials he was often as much the student as the lecturer. He learned from you and you learned from him. He was fascinated by other people's experience.
>
> I remember once that I did a mock exam while I was at Ruskin ... I was so frustrated that I couldn't say what I wanted that I stormed out. Ralph chased me down Walton Street, but he couldn't catch me. When I got back there was a note on my desk ... telling me not to worry and to come and have a talk ... He was always supportive like that.
>
> (Prescott, *The Guardian*, 11 December 1996)

The sheer humanity of the man shines through in Prescott's heartfelt testimony. Samuel's former colleagues were equally effusive in their praise for a much-loved and respected colleague. Fellow historian Carolyn Steedman wrote this warm tribute:

> The extent of his empathy was exceptional. No one charted more exactly the ways in which the Industrial Revolution had increased the extent of toil in every branch of Victorian industry ... His insights were the product of an omnivorous intellectual appetite, which crossed disciplines and periods: Samuel wrote with the insights of a literary critic, the acuity of an anthropologist and the wit of a political journalist.
>
> (Steedman, *Radical Philosophy*, March 1997)

Moving on to Samuel's pedagogical ideas, Steedman continues:

> He produced his historical work in interaction with working-class adult returners to education ... The standard charge against the history Samuel inspired was of a fanatical empiricism and a romantic merging of historians and their subjects in crowded narratives ... in which each hard-won detail of working class lives, wrenched from the cold indifference of posterity, is piled upon another, in a relentless rescue of the past. When he was himself subject to these charges, it was presumably his fine accounts of the labour process that critics had in mind. But it was meaning rather than minutiae that he cared about.
>
> (ibid.)

Gareth Stedman Jones, a highly respected historian in his own right, added his own thoughts on the exceptional contribution to the discipline of history by his old friend:

> Raphael Samuel's lasting memorials will be the work he inspired in the generations of students he taught at Ruskin College, Oxford, from 1962 to 1996, and History Workshop, in its protean forms of annual conferences, local networks and federations – which spread across Europe and Scandinavia – and its eponymous journal.
>
> (Stedman Jones, *The Independent*, 11 December 1996)

Following Samuel's death, the University of East London established The Raphael Samuel History Centre. The centre continues the work started by its founder, focusing in particular on the history of work, poverty, and immigration patterns in east London. In his specialist subject and in education more generally, Raphael Samuel's influence was and remains immense. He made a profound and enduring contribution to the history and development of Ruskin College and to adult learning more generally. His contention that education should have a dialectical and organic relationship with social movements is controversial and was as deeply unpopular on the political Right during Samuel's own time as it is today, but his legacy survives at Ruskin and its sister institutions such as the Mary Ward Centre and the Working Men's College.

From this necessarily brief account of the Selbourne/Samuel ideological rumpus it would appear that Samuel and the progressives won hands down. The Sloman Committee, set up to investigate the affair, concluded that the college was in breach of Selbourne's academic freedom for allowing students to disrupt lectures. Selbourne was simply unable to teach. In time he won his case against the college for wrongful dismissal, but was soon gone. His fêted opponent stayed and strengthened his standing at the college, before moving to set up a new research centre among the most disadvantaged communities of London. If only it were that simple. If the Left won the social and educational argument of the 1980s, Selbourne and his neo-liberal supporters triumphed in the longer term.

Following the Ruskin students' strike of 1909, the notion of a separate or independent working-class education began to diminish in strength and purpose. The increasing reach and effectiveness of the WEA, with its highly regarded three-year tutorial programme, mounted a serious challenge to specialist adult institutions such as Ruskin. On the Left in the 1970s persistent claims for notions of community and single-issue politics over rigid class distinctions began to dominate. In 1970, Ruskin College, perhaps recognizing the need to adapt, hosted the first women's liberation movement. Later in the 1970s, the college's students demonstrated in support of the republican movement in Northern Ireland. In 1984 staff and students showed their support for the striking miners (Thatcher's 'enemy within') and the attack on their communities by a merciless Tory government presiding over soaring unemployment, high interest rates, and industrial decline. In education, issues of gender, sexual politics, disability, and race seemed to gain in urgency over fading ideas about social class. Ruskin needed to take stock and reconsider its mission. In the last 30 years of the twentieth century, clamorous voices at the college and beyond questioned its founding purpose. How could a publicly funded residential centre for educating trade union leaders and Labour Party activists possibly survive in a hostile political environment?

In fast-changing times, some kept the faith. Left-wing political figures such as Arthur Scargill and Mick McGahey of the Communist Party of Great Britain (CPGB) stayed loyal to their beliefs, but began to appear like yesterday's men – rather than the heroic socialist revolutionaries they might have been in previous times. What Samuel described as 'radical chic' found a home in Eurocommunism, the Social Democratic Party, or *Marxism Today*, as sympathy drained away from centuries-old class commitments. Loudly hammering the final nail in the socialist coffin, Tony Blair and his New Labour Party dramatically struck Clause 4 from the Party's Constitution. David Selbourne played the long game and his 'third way' political and social analysis was attractive to liberals and 'champagne socialists' alike, while the organized hard-core Left epitomized by the group around *The Morning Star* has all but disappeared from the political scene. In an endnote to this brief account of the political controversy that engulfed Ruskin on two occasions in the twentieth century, a sign of the defeat of the socialist cause in the UK was the British Communist Party abandoning its hammer and sickle motif for a more conciliatory hammer and dove. The game was up.

Ruskin's claims for uniqueness have been weakened as a result of these political and cultural developments. Unlike its sister centres dedicated to adult learning, Ruskin is the only one of its kind to have had the explicit aim of preparing representatives of trade unions and Labour Party members for higher office. In later years, under the severest pressure, the college has broadened its initial purpose and is now, aside from its students living in, hardly distinguishable from those other institutions. In their brief history of Ruskin, *Ruskin College: Contesting knowledge, dissenting politics* (Andrews *et al.*, 1999), compiled to mark the college centenary, the authors claim that Ruskin has never had one fixed single purpose, but has, throughout its history, successfully managed to adapt to the changing times. This argument is somewhat disingenuous as it's clear that the founders were most interested in providing their students with a political education rather than anything more general. The college may continue to be successful, but not in its original defining sense.

Ruskin's shifting sense of mission over the past 30 years has been accompanied by a loss of influence on adult education nationally. An early indication was the failure to be invited onto the group that produced Bob Fryer's 1997 'Report into Adult Education'. The fact that the group included representatives from UNISON and Fircroft College was a further sign of Ruskin's diminished status. Free to disregard the historical conscience of adult learning, the report carefully avoided using social class as one of its central values, preferring instead less contentious notions such as community, lifelong learning, outreach, and social exclusion. Social justice remained at the heart of the report, but no mention was made of class struggle. As Jane Thompson remarked, 'Class solidarity and class struggle no longer carry much weight at Ruskin or elsewhere.' (ibid.: 132)

To be fair, Ruskin itself had moved on from its original inspiration years before 1997. Class struggle had ceased to provide the driving force for Ruskin long before Fryer's deliberations found their way into the Headington senior common room. Like society in general, particularly since the miners' defeat in 1984 and the deletion of Clause 4, the world has moved away from class struggle, even if poverty, alienation, and exploitation persist in all their forms to remind us of former battles. Certainly, today's Ruskin students have little connection or even awareness of the college's controversial past. If Ruskin College has lost its unique purpose of supporting the class struggle, what does it stand for today? What constitutes a successful Ruskin student in the modern era if it's no longer to become an active trade union representative or Labour leader?

I was privileged to work with a group of ten Ruskin students on my three-day visit to the Headington campus in October 2013. The group were happy to share their experiences of being an adult residential student and to talk about their hopes and aspirations for the future. The college also allowed me access to its archive of student profiles, which afforded me a more extensive range of research material. The ten students I met were studying a broad range of courses including English, history, social work training, creative writing and critical practice, and writing for performance at both diploma and degree level. Virtually all of the group had a negative and unhappy experience of school and were keen to put this right. They included women in low-level care positions desperate to become fully qualified social workers, together with amateur poets and writers who were following a dream. An example of the latter was a soldier-poet, Steve, who turned to writing to help him overcome the horrors he experienced in war-torn Bosnia. Steve is now studying at Ruskin for a degree in creative writing.

One of the Ruskin students I was privileged to meet was a member of a small group who go proudly by the name of the Ransackers. They follow a short, ten-week introductory research course prior to registering for a degree. Adrian was excluded from school on ten occasions. One of a family of eight children, he was brought up on a tough south London council estate where he learned to fend for himself and acquired a kind of streetwise independence. As a boy he loved reading, despite everything his schools did to discourage him. Adrian's love of language eventually got him into Ruskin to study creative writing. His writing flourished in the residential setting and he is now at Keele University studying for a degree in script-writing.

Ransackers like Adrian have at least one thing in common: they share tremendous resolve to transform their lives through study. Their presence at Ruskin is an emphatic endorsement of the college's mission and evolving philosophy of education. A few of the group are acutely aware of the college's proud past, while most remain oblivious to what might appear to the modern adult student as irrelevant, esoteric debates of an earlier age. But, as we shall see, the Ransackers have a direct lineage to their nineteenth-century forebears. Performance poet Rowan Padmore knew she had to make sacrifices to fulfil her dream of studying creative writing in Oxford:

> I gave up my job, my home and gave away all my furniture and
> possessions to study at Ruskin. I am so pleased that I did. I live in a
> single study bedroom with just the books I need for the course and
> a few other bits and pieces. I have found it all strangely liberating.
>
> (Padmore, www.ruskin.ac.uk, accessed April 2014)

Rowan performs at local poetry events and is a student governor at the college. Like the early Ruskin students, her student experience changed her life, but it is doubtful whether her predecessors achieved transformation through performance poetry. They would more likely have been shop stewards from the mining or railway industries learning about negotiation or collective bargaining rather than the techniques of modern theatre. This may be a crude comparison but it is an indication of how Ruskin has adapted to political and cultural change over the past century.

David Tanguay lives a 30-minute drive from Oxford but chose to take up a residency so he could concentrate fully on his studies. This determined 73-year-old began with the Ransackers course, spending his ten weeks compiling a 10,000-word dissertation. After successfully completing his introductory course, David is now studying at Ruskin for a history degree. To leave his family and his beloved allotment for ten weeks at a time to pursue his passion illustrates the commitment and dedication of Ruskin's residential students. Like the illustrious John Prescott, our history undergraduate was once a merchant seaman and both men were former members of the Marine Society's College of the Sea, who provided a book box in every port. But unlike Prescott today, David prefers to live a more quiet life.

Bill Haywood attended Ruskin between 1973 and 1976. He left school at 15 with no formal qualifications and 21 years later attended Ruskin and gained his first diploma. His life was changed forever. Bill's memoir, *On Life's Little Twists and Turns*, published in April 2014, tells the story of his journey from factory floor to seminar room. A working-class lad from the Black Country, Bill joined the Forces serving in Cyprus and Malta. A few years later, free from military service, he joined one of the largest engineering companies in the UK. At the age of 36, like Harding's Jude Fawley, Bill threw caution to the winds and left his factory job to pursue his dream of a university education. Three years later, with his degree safely secured, he began studying for the doctorate he eventually achieved at the age of 45. It is a remarkable story of courage, resolve, and success – ironically, all cherished Victorian values so dear to the heart of the current Tory policymakers.

Bill is in a long line of mature students who, through their own efforts, escaped a life of drudgery and frustration (what Marx described as alienation) and reinvented themselves. We saw this with that proud autodidact Malcolm Williams and now, 30 years later, with Bill Haywood.

Adrienne is a different case. A pensioner, she returned to learning because she was bored with retirement and wanted a new challenge. She is typical of many pensioners who want a more interesting life that provides testing experiences and intellectual stimulation. This is Adrienne's extraordinary story:

LIKE BEING GIVEN WINGS

My first foray into adult education as a mature student was in my early 30s. But I failed to complete the six years of an OU degree. I thought I'll never go back to studying again. By the time I returned to education, I was 30 years older. As I write this, it's three days since I celebrated my sixty-ninth birthday. When I retired at 60 I had no thought of going back to studying. However, my husband brought home a leaflet about the Ransackers Project at Ruskin College. I took the plunge. At my interview the two staff who chatted to me very informally accepted me to undertake research on the experiences of refugee women in the UK.

That first week in January 2009 was purgatory. If I had gone home then I would not have returned. But fear of the unknown quickly gave way to excitement. We had superb support from tutors used to dealing with people returning to education after a lengthy gap. The day we went to the Bodleian library for the historic process of joining, providing access to the libraries of all the Oxford Colleges, was, for me, like being given wings.

By the end of the three months I was so bitten by the education bug that I signed up for another three-month stint, this time as an independent student. The subject again focused on immigration. My 8,000 words were about very young children held in UK immigration removal centres, something I had not discovered during my previous Ransackers session. I learned a lot about the experiences of immigrants, both in the UK and around the world, and I am proud that my first essay, which branded the UK Border Agency (UKBA) as unwieldy and unworkable, turned into reality when the Home Secretary, Theresa May, admitted that the UKBA was 'too large, secretive and unaccountable'.

> Adult education is about providing ways to feed the mind, answering questions, posing new ones, and turning stunted growth into healthy plants. I am somewhat astonished to find myself almost at the end of an Open University degree in international studies. It is only in relating my experiences that I am able to recognize how much my adult education has changed me.
>
> What's next? I am hoping to finish my degree with a creative writing module and maybe finish the novel I started ten years ago, just before I retired. Guess what it is about? Between you and me, one of the main characters is an asylum seeker. At 60-plus my world opened up, instead of starting to close down. The belated opportunity to study has helped me recognize what I am passionate about. I have learned that not only is the world far more complex than I had ever realized but it is also far more interesting.

Adrienne is clearly an extremely able person who has unfailing family support. Her Ransackers course gave her the confidence to try for a degree with the OU that she is close to completing. We look forward to reading her novel when it comes out, as I am sure it will.

The Ruskin residential experience enabled Adrian, David, Bill, and Adrienne to realize their previously unfulfilled potential. They are part of an ongoing tradition of mature students studying at Ruskin that began back in the heady days of the 1890s. As I write, the college has nearly 1,500 part-time and 70 full-time students, 86 per cent of whom are from outside Oxford. One of them, former student Frances Cage, talked about her own Ruskin experience:

> It has been the most wonderful experience and I am going away with my head full of ideas and memories, and with many new friends. I have learned that it is never too late to study or to learn, but without this opportunity, and all the terrific facilities Ruskin and Oxford have offered, I would never have known. How can I ever describe studying in the Bodleian library? I am proud to be called a Ransacker!

In June 2014 the General Secretary of the TUC, Frances O'Grady, gave an address to the students and staff at Ruskin College. In the course of her talk, O'Grady described Ruskin as the 'intellectual hub of the working class'. This is a bold statement that may have been accurate in the days when John Prescott and other eminent Labour Party members made up the majority of the student population at Ruskin. The college can no longer claim to be the stronghold of working-class radicalism, if it ever could – the old British Community Party probably had greater claim to be the centre of working-class intellectual life. Today's Ruskin students are a remarkably diverse group, but no longer the blue-collar students of the previous generation, or as imagined by the General Secretary of the TUC. Today's students do not see themselves as the subjects of messianic zeal on the part of the college teaching staff. Modern students are far too independent to be patronized and, in any case, do not usually represent anybody other than themselves. This is not a criticism of Ruskin, which continues to do an excellent job at the heart of adult learning in the UK:

> Powerful leadership and the drive and dedication of staff enable students at Ruskin to make tremendous progress.
>
> (Ofsted Report, 2012)

Professor Audrey Mullender, now retired as principal of Ruskin, oversaw the controversial move to Headington from the original site in downtown Oxford, a handsome building in Walton Street acquired from wealthy St John's. Professor Mullender justified the move to the local newspaper:

> We are excited and exhilarated by our move into the beautifully redeveloped premises at our site in Old Headington, which should be fit for the twenty-first century, and look forward to offering second-chance educational opportunities to many more people for at least another century to come.
>
> Although we treasure all the memories and the wonderful work that has taken place at our Walton Street site and all the lives that have been changed by the students that have been educated there, we recognize the site in its present state cannot accommodate the needs of our students, particularly disabled people. It needs a great deal of money spend on it.
>
> (*Oxford Times*, 28 September 2012)

The move to Headington in 2012 was controversial, as these things always are, but the sale to Exeter College of the Walton Street building enabled the purchase of the Headington site and a recent £17 million redevelopment. The move has been vindicated by a significant increase in enrolments, an expansion of the programme, and a much-needed improvement in facilities. With the new Callaghan Library, modern lecture rooms, free parking, and impressive student accommodation, the college has certainly moved with the times, as Professor Mullender claims. The current students do complain a little about being so far from the city centre action, but the distracting delights of Oxford are just a short bus ride away.

Figure 9: The proud new home of Ruskin in the leafy suburb of Headington. Today's students enjoy modern teaching and library facilities, but may miss the excitement of their former central Oxford location. (With special thanks to photographer Stuart Maidment.)

If the young American founders, Beard and Vrooman, envisaged a college where working men could become better, more politically aware citizens, today's students are as likely to be pensioners, ex-military personnel, care workers, women returners, writers, and poets, or people using education to recover from dependency or mental health problems. Many of them believe they have a point to prove following a damaging school experience, or for the first time in their adult lives they are free from family responsibilities. Ruskin continues to provide training opportunities for trade union representatives, and the socialist cause remains etched on the soul of the place, but this element of their programme no longer dominates as it once did. It is a dramatic change that reflects the cultural revolution of the past 50 years. Managers and governors at Ruskin understand the new demographic, and it is a tribute to the college that it has retained its relevance to adults with such diverse social and educational needs as feminism, diversity, and environmental issues, which dominate the agenda for guest lectures and open days. Ruskin College may no longer be the 'intellectual hub of the working class', but it continues to hold on to its special place at the heart of adult learning and remains a living embodiment of the history of adult education in the UK.

Chapter 5

A higher calling

A liberating experience

The real heroes of adult learning are not celebrated intellectuals or the authors of its sacred texts but the thousands of students who, for a host of reasons, return to learning each year. Some are content with a short course in pottery, yoga, or one of the hundreds of activities available in schools, adult centres, and draughty village halls the length and breadth of the country. Students, or in contemporary jargon, 'learners' and even worse 'funding units', arrive to follow a dream, find spiritual nourishment, upgrade their skills, or just discover how their digital camera or computer works. Some of this they can access online, but most prefer the human contact and conviviality provided by a regular class. There are others, perhaps more determined and ambitious, who look to take their studies to a higher level. These brave souls follow their educational star where it leads them. It might be the Open University or one of the many HE colleges providing degree-level study, some exclusively for mature students. These determined souls owe their opportunities not to David Selbourne, Raphael Samuel, Richard Hoggart, or Raymond Williams but to the nineteenth-century scientist and benefactor George Birkbeck.

The adult college that carries his name sits proudly in central London a short walk across Russell Square from the Mary Ward Centre. Leave Trafalgar Square and set off east along the Strand for a couple of hundred yards past the centuries-old Crown and Anchor Tavern, to which we will return. Leave the river on your right and turn left into the delights of Covent Garden, now selling expensive clothes and designer jewellery rather than the apples and pears of the old market. Pause for a moment to listen to buskers playing Vivaldi, who have replaced the organ grinder's monkey as street entertainment. After a couple of minutes leave the tourists behind and wander through the inspiring public spaces of the Royal Opera House and out into High Holborn. Cross one of the busiest thoroughfares in the capital and enter Bloomsbury. Once the cultural heart of Britain, the district is now dominated by the sprawling campus of London University and the much-loved British Museum. This rather unfashionable quarter of the capital is where writers, painters, and philosophers such as Virginia Woolf, John

Philip Stevens

Maynard Keynes, and Lytton Strachey lived and worked in the early part of the twentieth century. Their legacy seems to hang in the air. It permeates the corridors of Senate House, where their portraits gaze down as a reminder of the decisive contribution the Bloomsbury Set made to the cultural and political life of the capital.

Figure 10: In this exquisite engraving by F. Maurer (1753), the Crown and Anchor (on the corner at right) stands next to St Clement's Church. Later home to nineteenth-century radicals, the pub hosted the launch of Dr George Birkbeck's London Mechanics' Institute. (By kind permission of the London Metropolitan Archive.)

To describe the grounds of London University as a campus is somewhat of a euphemism. The university occupies most of the streets stretching from Russell Square to Euston Road, taking in some of the most delightful Georgian squares in the capital. For good or bad, the university has taken over this part of the London Borough of Camden. Among its academic glories are King's College, Imperial College, the School of Oriental and African Studies, and, arguably the world's premier teacher-training establishment, the Institute of Education in Bedford Way. In the 1980s I had the good fortune to attend an aesthetics class in the basement of a delightful Georgian terrace in Woburn Square conducted by that inspirational teacher of philosophy Ray Elliot. Today the terrace houses part of the university's Business School.

But it would be wrong to think of Bloomsbury as unvaryingly prosperous or exclusively academic. As we saw in the previous chapter,

Camden is one of the capital's most ethnically diverse boroughs. The estates tucked away behind the British Museum are full of Bengali families living in overcrowded and cramped conditions whose lives are challenged every day by social, cultural, and economic poverty. Nothing could be further from the bohemian Bloomsbury ideal than life in these bleak inner-city high-rises. The Mary Ward Centre, the British Museum community team, and other local groups work with great imagination to ensure these communities do not become isolated from their well-heeled neighbours on the other side of the museum. This part of Camden not only has persistent problems with poverty, health, and housing, but the area has also experienced appalling tragedy. Close to Russell Square underground station is a popular Italian café. On the morning of 7 July 2005, the café became a temporary field hospital where those injured in the terrorist attack were treated with some dignity, away from the mayhem let loose on the streets outside.

Situated at the heart of the university's property empire, just a few yards away from the monolithic Senate House – described rather unkindly by Fred Inglis as 'Soviet like' in its architecture – is the destination of our gentle stroll through the heart of London, Birkbeck College. Step through the electronic doors of the dazzling new glass entrance into the reception area and you might think you have wandered into one of the many four-star hotels that grace this part of London. To the left of the entrance sits a bank of computers and an elongated reception desk staffed by porters attired smartly in the college's corporate livery. A couple of years ago, prior to the refurbishment, students entered Birkbeck through the Malet Street entrance, beside which stands the most glorious magnolia in London. The tree has survived in all its glory, but the homely old entrance has disappeared. The college has successfully moved with the times, but has lost something of the musty appeal of the old place. But I am sure George Birkbeck would have approved of the modernization.

Yorkshire-born Birkbeck was a highly respected physician who was determined to provide educational opportunities in science and technology to working-class people, in itself a revolutionary ideal in the nineteenth century. Early in his career, Birkbeck practised in Glasgow where he established hugely popular science classes attended by over 500 people. The demand was overwhelming and convinced Birkbeck that skilled workers had a real thirst for scientific knowledge and were keen to contribute to the rapidly changing face of industry. When he moved south later in his career, Birkbeck decided to repeat his Glasgow experiment in London. This now-eminent physician could not have imagined how successful his new venture would become.

Soon after he arrived in the capital, Birkbeck set about gathering together a group of like-minded liberals who would help him with his project. Leading figures of the day quickly gave their support. Utilitarian Jeremy Bentham, economist David Ricardo, philosopher J.S. Mill, political radical and classicist Walter Grote, and social reformer Francis Place all quickly signed up to the physician's passionate plea for help. Encouraged by such enthusiasm for his idea, on 11 November 1823 Birkbeck arranged a public meeting at the Crown and Anchor Tavern. The meeting was an outstanding success. The following day *The Star* reported:

> ... more than two thousand persons must have been present, among them 'numbers of respectable mechanics'.

The get-together at the old hostelry on that November evening in 1823 was effectively the beginning of the nationwide Mechanics' Institute movement. Birkbeck was invited to take the chair and a management committee was elected who quickly set about writing a constitution. The committee was made up of engineers, tailors, shoemakers, and men from the oil industry and construction. Birkbeck was absolutely adamant that workers should not only be represented on the committee but should be encouraged to form a majority. A general meeting of the new association was held at the same Strand pub on 2 December, where, as historian C. Delisle Burns wrote:

> At this General Meeting ... the first phase of the development of Birkbeck College began when the London Mechanics Institute was declared to be then and there founded.
>
> (Burns, 1924: 26)

A bold new educational experiment was up and running. The use of the word 'mechanic' is interesting, and central to the founder's educational philosophy. Dr Birkbeck believed in the intelligence of the working class, particularly the skilled tradesmen who had flocked to his Glasgow seminaries. He was also aware there was little in the way of educational opportunities available to working people at the time – Forster's 1870 Education Act was nearly 50 years away. For Birkbeck and his followers the consequence of this lack of educational opportunity was a tremendous thirst for knowledge among the 'aristocracy of labour' – skilled artisans who were aware of the technological and scientific change taking place in their industries and who wanted to be part of it. The term 'mechanic' was a catch-all for skilled workers right across industry. If 'mechanics' were his target group for the London initiative, Birkbeck also had clear ideas about how his new college should be governed, what should be taught, and who should do the teaching. That Birkbeck found time and energy to think through and implement a radical new experiment in workers' education and attend to a successful career in medicine is a tribute to the good doctor's energy and social conscience.

The first classes of the London Institute were held at the new headquarters in Southampton Place on the edge of Bloomsbury and at the popular Monkwell Street Chapel. Birkbeck wanted to provide his students with the best possible education and although most tutors were volunteers at the start, payment was introduced once the college became established. The governors produced a journal, *The London Mechanics Magazine* (later to become *The Lodestone* and, more recently, the *Birkbeck Magazine*), which helped to spread the word across the capital. This early form of marketing did its job – within a few years Mechanics' Institutes were created in Spitalfields, Hackney, Deptford, Rotherhithe, and Bermondsey, all inner-city working-class communities. As Birkbeck's biographer wrote:

> The movement spread in all parts of England and at most of these new Institutions the members looked for suggestions and inspiration to Dr Birkbeck and to the foundation which now bears his name.
>
> (Burns, 1924: 38)

Consistent with the founder's radical vision, women were admitted as students in 1830, although not all members of the committee were enthusiastic. For some unexplained reason women were allowed to attend lectures but not classes. Some even questioned 'the propriety of admitting females through the front entrance'. The separate registers that were kept for female students reveal they travelled to central London all the way from Clapham, Hoxton, Battersea, and as far out as Dulwich and Harrow. Did they come alone? Did they walk, or travel by public transport? Either way, their journey would not have been easy. The London Underground didn't open until 1863, although horse-drawn buses were available in central London from as early as 1829. We don't know the answer to these questions, but we do know that women were prepared to go to great lengths to attend the institute lectures. Despite their strong reservations about women members, the committee did grant them full library membership and several of the outstanding women students won coveted essay prizes, but not fellowships, which were strictly for men.

Within a few years, Birkbeck became the first choice for adult students who wanted a university education but who couldn't afford to study full time. An indication of the success of the project was that 1,300 'mechanics' attended the early classes, while over 1,000 paid their subscriptions (*The*

Examiner, 19 February 1824). These were numbers the founders could hardly have imagined. The foundations had been laid. Of course, in the early nineteenth century, Birkbeck's visionary initiative did not escape criticism. The doctor's pioneering radicalism was hard won and faced considerable opposition from the beginning. Opponents argued that educating working men and women was fraught with danger. Given the revolutionary events in Europe at this time, detractors claimed that knowledge would raise consciousness and almost certainly turn students into political agitators bent on revolution. The *St James Chronicle* went on the attack:

> A scheme more completely adapted for destruction of the empire could not have been invented.
>
> (quoted in Burns, 1924: 27)

Later in the article the writer accused Birkbeck and his friends of 'scattering the seeds of evil' and spreading a 'tissue of vile bombast' (May 1825). Ouch! This reaction was fairly predictable and would not have deterred such a determined group of people. More encouraging was an article in *The Examiner* in support of the Mechanics' Institute:

> When revolution is brought about it will be managed in a very different way from what we have seen in Italy and Spain; it will be signalled by temperance and wisdom, and encounter no risk of reaction from want of policy or experience.
>
> (quoted in Burns, 1924: 25)

Other criticism was less predictable. From his lofty intellectual perch, Thomas Carlyle argued that the 'steam intellect' society promoted by George Birkbeck and friends was grossly inferior to the classical education found in the ancient universities of Oxford and Cambridge. Carlyle hated the Industrial Revolution and the progress of science and its attempt to 'destroy mystery'. Some of the topics taught in the early days would certainly not have been to the great critic's taste. The *Mechanics Magazine* of 1838–9 lists the three Autumn Lectures as:

1. On the manufacture of silk worm gut.
2. On the strength of steam boiler materials
3. On the essential qualities of good guns.

Choosing such hard-core science subjects tells us that Birkbeck was deadly serious about the teaching of the subject. He was a scientist at the very heart. However, he had developed clear ideas about education, one of the aims of which was to 'humanize' his students rather than provide them with a purely technical education. The great man brushed off all opposition as his London venture grew from strength to strength. One of the most interesting things about the Yorkshireman was that he combined compassion for working people with a radical philosophy of higher education. In his history of the Birkbeck College, Burns describes the founder's educational ideas as 'heuristic':

> The history of Birkbeck College has a special 'heuristic' value for higher education. By 'heuristic' ... I mean the quality of suggesting a fresh method of development, capable of yet further application.
>
> (Burns, 1924: 5)

Burns breaks this 'heuristic value' into two component parts. First:

> What was originally an institution for general popular education has been made to grow from being a place where it has become a living whole of the university standard.
>
> (Burns, 1924: 5)

Burns's second point is far more radical:

> A large part of the motive force which impelled the transition could be derived from the students themselves. Rarely have undergraduates made an effort with so direct a purpose of raising the intellectual status of their College, or with so definite an outcome, as have the students of Birkbeck College.
>
> (Burns, 1924: 5)

From this germ of an idea, George Birkbeck had created educational opportunities for working-class adults where there were none before. In addition, he insisted that the workers themselves had direct involvement in the management and governance of the institute. Not content with this remarkable achievement, Birkbeck's democratic impulse extended into teaching and learning and into the classroom itself. The core subjects at the institute were science, mathematics, and economics – not the literary or cultural studies favoured by more recent thinkers about adult learning. Introducing experimental teaching methods into physics, for example, was not without risk. But there was something more to Burns's 'heuristic' claims for the Mechanics' Institute that facilitated good teaching. The process of teaching and learning was mediated by respect for the students' views and experiences and by a negotiated curriculum. Through this process the institute achieved a skilful balance between maintaining high standards while fostering a democratic classroom. Nearly 170 years later Raphael Samuel and others introduced the same principle at Ruskin College to dramatic effect.

Birkbeck's reflective but firm leadership took the institute into unchartered territory and ahead of Oxford and Cambridge in the teaching of biology and chemistry. The success of the institute was achieved on limited funds and the minimum of equipment. In December 1824 the committee minutes reported an order for 'two dozen books and two dozen slates for the Thursday Arithmetic class'.

As we have seen, the first tutors at the institute were volunteers, but Birkbeck argued that paying staff would encourage a more professional ethos. Paying tutors provided a model for others to follow but had serious implications for the institute's finances. Birkbeck's committee faced a critical choice. Did they rely on donations from external benefactors – well-meaning middle-class liberals – to balance the books, or should they stick to their principles and make the institute self-funding? Could the institute survive on students' subscriptions alone? These fundamental questions split the founders. Birkbeck argued that survival would be extremely difficult without additional funding, but some of his colleagues reminded him that:

> If the founders had agreed in the terms of their original proposal
> that the workers 'must not depend on charity but on themselves;
> they must pay for instruction'.
>
> (Burns, 1924: 32)

Birkbeck may have been a visionary but he was pragmatic when necessary. He knew that without government or local authority support the project would not survive on student subscriptions alone. Not for the first time the founder won the argument and £3,000 was raised in charitable donations to fund a new lecture theatre, opened in July 1825 by the Duke of Sussex. The committee had reached a working compromise, although relationships between the members became strained to breaking point. Writing nearly 100 years later, Burns believed that:

> The disagreement is significant; for it turned upon the principles
> of democratic education and is somewhat like our contemporary
> controversy on adult education between the Workers' Educational
> Association and the Plebs League.
>
> (Burns, 1924: 30)

We can now see that the seeds of the Ruskin dispute in 1911 were sown in the previous century by George Birkbeck and his team. Birkbeck refused to give an inch in protecting the original democratic impulse. Students sat on all institute committees and retained a major influence in its affairs. Of course, the Mechanics' Institute was only partly self-governing, but a higher education institution with any degree of self-governance in the nineteenth century contrasted sharply with the elitism of Oxford and Cambridge. Neither the committee nor the students saw any contradiction between democratic control and high academic standards. Here was the essence of Birkbeck's educational experiment: a radical curriculum designed for working people, and democratic governance and management, together with the highest standards of teaching and learning.

But first students needed to be recruited. Notices were sent directly to factories and workplaces advertising the 'practical' courses available at the institute in order to attract 'mechanics', the committee's target group. The first edition of the *Birkbeck Institution Magazine* appeared on 1 September 1892 (price 1 penny) with four pages of advertisements to boost revenue. Products advertised included Thomson's Corsets, Holloway's Pills and Ointments, and, interestingly, the Birkbeck Bank.

In order not to put off potential students or antagonize employers, the committee took care to avoid any reference to theory or ideas in the programme notes. However, mathematics, science, and economics hardly provided vocational training that employers at that time were beginning to provide in-house. By the end of the nineteenth century, major companies such as Tate & Lyle and Bryant and May in east London started to introduce social and cultural clubs for employees at their factories in Canning Town and Wapping. But the Mechanics' Institute differed from these welcome initiatives in that it offered degree-level study for working men and, a few years later, working women.

So, who were the people willing to pay a hard-earned 6 shillings membership and 2 shillings and sixpence to attend classes following a long shift at work? And importantly, what were the entry requirements for the institute at a time when most working-class people were denied even the most rudimentary education? From the beginning, Birkbeck targeted the skilled working class as Burns confirms:

> ... the College provides ... for the higher educational needs of those who are making their living while they increase their knowledge and their skills in the art of life.
>
> (Burns, 1924: 15)

The 'labour aristocracy' came in numbers:

> They were skilled craftsmen, more closely connected socially and
> in economic and political interests with the shop-keeper and the
> 'middle' class than with the workers in those industries in which
> the new machines had become common.
>
> (Burns, 1924: 41–2)

The first students were relatively high earners and experienced in combination
and trade societies. The men who met that evening in 1823 in the Crown and
Anchor Tavern were, in the words of the institute's press releases, 'respectable
mechanics' who supported reform but remained loyal to the political order
– hardly the revolutionaries Birkbeck's opponents feared. The registers of the
first 20 years include details of the students' trades. Later in the nineteenth
century, occupational information ceased to be recorded and it was never
kept for women students. The members' register of 1882–4, the last to show
employment information, tells us that students were watchmakers, printers,
cabinet-makers, silversmith, and tailors, with an increasing number of clerks,
teachers, and merchants. We don't know the reason why occupational
information about students ceased to be kept after about 1888. Perhaps it
was because more lower-middle-class students began to attend the institute –
with fewer of the original target group: blue-collar 'mechanics'.

As the Industrial Revolution gathered pace, more and more workers
were thrown into menial work as the old skills were no longer required.
Machinery that dominated the cotton industry in Lancashire was soon
introduced into coal mines, the engineering industry in Birmingham, and the
docks and shipbuilding areas in London and the North East. The institute's
committee was faced with a dilemma, as Burns reveals:

> Three years after the Mechanics' Institute was founded, it became
> doubtful whether the persons deriving benefit from it were those
> for whom it was originally intended.
>
> (Burns, 1924: 43)

Birkbeck and his colleagues responded to the new machine age by redefining
the term 'working class', a familiar ploy:

> It comprehends all those members who work and do not employ
> journeymen.
>
> (Burns, 1924: 43)

As the old distinctions became blurred, Birkbeck's original vision began to be
compromised. But how could it be otherwise? The 'mechanics' he originally
targeted were beginning to disappear and few of the genuine working class

had the necessary entry requirements to undertake degree-level courses. This does not diminish Birkbeck's achievement. His London Mechanics' Institute was an outstanding success by any criteria. With just three principals in the first 95 years, the founder clearly enjoyed the loyalty of his staff. Through sheer determination, Birkbeck had established a pioneering educational project that grew in strength over the next two centuries to the point where its reputation spread across the world. In 1904 Sidney Webb described the institute as delivering, 'the kind of evening instruction for the intelligent workman that is unique in the world'. In a letter of apology for failing to attend Birkbeck's Centenary Dinner in 1924, the vice-chancellor of London University, H.J. Waring, wrote of his respect for Birkbeck's achievement:

> I do not know of a finer example in the annals of education of the perseverance over difficulties, which, but for the evidence … which lies on my desk, I should have described as insuperable.
>
> (letter from Waring, from the
> Birkbeck College archive, viewed 13 May 2014)

In 1907 the Mechanics' Institute changed its name to Birkbeck College and six years later Lord Haldane recommended the institute be made a constituent college of the University of London. This was formalized in 1920 when Birkbeck became a School of the University, dedicated to the teaching of evening and part-time students. In 1952 the college moved to its current home in Malet Street in the heart of Bloomsbury. Over the twentieth century the college has added departments in psychology, crystallography, history, languages, geology, politics, sociology, law, and business to its founding subjects of mathematics, science, and economics. Dr George Birkbeck's early nineteenth-century vision has been well and truly realized in ways he could never have imagined.

The college has continued to expand and in 2003 the Princess Royal opened a £20 million extension at Malet Street, enabling Birkbeck to offer over 1,000 certificate and diploma courses and undergraduate degrees, together with around 90 postgraduate and research opportunities. The founders would have thoroughly approved of the opening of the Birkbeck Institute for Lifelong Learning in 2004, as the founder's vision began to spread across the capital. In partnership with the University of East London, the college opened an outreach centre in Stratford. Around one in four Birkbeck students come from an ethnic minority, 14 per cent of all undergraduates have no formal qualifications on entry, and over 95 per cent of all students are aged 25 or over. If all of these developments are consistent with the values of the old London Mechanics' Institute, I'm not sure what the founders would have thought about the Clore Management Centre, which opened in 1997, a formidable-looking edifice just across the square from the main building. But they would have approved of the excellence research results achieved by the college across all its departments.

Birkbeck's alumni include social reformers Annie Besant and Sydney Webb, Labour Prime Minister Ramsey MacDonald, Chief Executive of the UK Supreme Court Jenny Rowe, and peace activist Samir El-Youssef. Lord Haldane, Dr Armitage Smith, Dr George Senter, Professor George Overend, and Baroness Blackstone were all former Masters of the College. Distinguished former staff include the biologist J.D. Bernal, historian Nikolaus Pevsner, socialist historian Eric Hobsbawm, DNA specialist Rosalind Franklin, and philosopher Roger Scruton.

Today's Birkbeck students enjoy the opportunities provided by the founders of the original institute, and the hundreds who enrol each September are direct descendents from the 'mechanics' who showed up that cold December evening at the Crown and Anchor, and who later flocked to classes at the Monkwell Street Chapel. If we look at the college today and speak to some of the students we can trace the connections to that cold winter's evening in London's West End.

As mentioned, in the formative years women were allowed limited access to the Mechanics' Institute. But things were soon to change as Raymond Williams's 'long revolution' began to pick up pace. At the time that women began to attend in greater numbers in the late nineteenth century, sharp-elbowed merchants, clerks, teachers, and lawyers started to replace genuine working-class artisans, for whom the institute was originally established. This trend grew in strength through the twentieth century. The radical education experiment, with its modest beginnings in a London pub, had been hijacked by the upwardly mobile London middle class. But all is not lost. Today there are encouraging signs that George Birkbeck's original educational vision is again showing signs of life. The student population at Birkbeck has changed dramatically. Williams's 'revolution' has not only resulted in a hard-won change in attitudes towards women, but by a shifting demographic that has almost obliterated the old industrial working class. Fluid immigration patterns in London and all major British cities has brought with it attendant problems of poverty, homelessness, and prejudice. If this were not difficult enough, adult learning providers have had to respond to the complex educational needs of students, some with mental health problems, some trafficked people, refugees, or those who have escaped from the horrors of war and terrorism. Birkbeck has faced these challenges with energy and imagination and the staff have worked extremely hard to meet the demands of this shifting demographic. They might envy the social and cultural certainties of their nineteenth-century forerunners.

Among the great successes at Birkbeck in recent years is the dramatic increase in the number of women students attending the college. In 2013–14, 50 per cent of Birkbeck students were women, a welcome correction to the derisory low participation rates of the nineteenth century. At the college today, women follow a broad range of subjects at all levels from certificate to postgraduate study. Among the many courageous women who overcame prejudice and disadvantage to succeed at Birkbeck was Dr Mia Kellmer Pringle, whose achievements are highlighted by Jane Humber in her *Daily Mail* article 'A Woman's View'. As Humber tells us, Pringle was born into a comfortable Viennese middle-class family in 1929. Her mother managed to escape persecution while her father, an active socialist, was less fortunate and perished in a Nazi concentration camp. Humber continues:

> Mia and her mother arrived in Britain with only the clothes they were wearing and it was the misery she saw among uprooted children … that made her vow to dedicate her life to the betterment of their situation.
>
> (*Daily Mail*, 7 June 1982)

Pringle was employed as a chambermaid and later as a shop assistant at Woolworth's. Following a series of evening classes in shorthand and typing this determined young woman became a secretary and then, one evening, she heard Birkbeck College mentioned on the radio and her life changed forever. In 1941 Mia enrolled on an evening postgraduate diploma before taking on the challenging academic demands of a doctorate in psychology. After a few years teaching in primary schools, Mia qualified as an educational and clinical psychologist. In 1963 Dr Pringle founded the National Children's Bureau, which quickly grew into a highly influential body with 75 staff.

The Bureau pioneered the concept of 'children's advocate', undertook extensive research, and raised the profile of children's rights and the importance of responsible parenting. Dr Pringle was later appointed president of the Pre-School Playgroup Association and consultant to UNICEF in Europe. Jane Humber was inspired to write Mia Pringle's story when she met the distinguished child psychologist at Hull University, where she was awarded an honorary DSc. Mia's achievement are, of course, remarkable and a tribute to her ambition, compassion, and sheer will-power. Birkbeck College gave her the opportunity to fulfil her considerable potential and the chance to achieve her extraordinary ambitions. In 1823 Mia would have been allowed to attend lectures but not classes, but over 100 years later, George Birkbeck's dream enabled a passionate young woman to change the world. Not all women students at Birkbeck achieve such giddy heights as Mia Kellmer Pringle. Some study to improve their English, advance their career prospects, or learn more about a much-loved subject, but all of their stories are as important as Mia's and all owe their opportunity to an indomitable Yorkshireman back in 1823.

Figure 11: Birkbeck College, 'London's Evening University', lights up the Bloomsbury skyline.

In May 2014 I met Caroline McDonald at a café just off Russell Square, a few hundred yards away from the main Birkbeck campus. Caroline has been Head of Outreach and Retention at the college for the past six years. We met to talk about her work and in particular about Birkbeck's new outpost in Stratford. In 2004, before any decision had been made about the London Olympics, Birkbeck was invited by the Higher Education Funding Council (HEFC) to discuss poor participation rates in higher education in east London. According to HEFC ward-by-ward research data, Newham had the lowest participation rates in the UK. Despite the efforts of the University of East London (UEL) and the Aimhigher project, the numbers remained scandalously low. UEL's traditional intake was 18–20 year olds and the HEFC wanted to raise expectations among an older demographic that might have aspirations to study. The HEFC were well aware of Birkbeck's impressive record with mature students and thought they might find a way to improve participation and, importantly, retention. After much discussion Birkbeck agreed to work with the HEFC and UEL on a joint project.

Despite initial progress being slow and discussions tricky, Birkbeck's first outreach centre was finally opened in 2006 and the first students arrived in September 2007. The Bloomsbury-based partner did not wish to replicate UEL's programme and after a period of intelligence gathering it was decided to focus on IT, languages, history, and community development. All subjects were initially taught to either certificate or foundation degree level, although a BSc in social science was introduced later as a progression route. In an impressive example of networking, Caroline's team developed close links with trade unions, LEAs, Sure Start groups, third sector organizations, and FE colleges in order to promote the work of the Stratford centre. A learning support unit was quickly set up at Stratford to provide help with special needs or language problems. In the first couple of years, the age profile of the new centre was around 35, about the same as the main campus. One of the more unexpected results of the initiative was a 25 per cent increase in the number of students from east London registering directly for courses at the main Bloomsbury site. The Birkbeck staff have worked tirelessly to establish the centre as a regular feature of daily life in the area. And there is little doubt that the Stratford initiative has made a significant contribution to meeting the educational needs of adults from east London

The gender balance across all programmes at Birkbeck is 50/50 and there is a new and growing trend in young adults choosing to study in the evenings while working during the day. With the recent introduction of a three-year evening degree, students can avoid the debt associated with the traditional route while gaining important work experience. To support them in their studies, Birkbeck offers students generous yearly cash bursaries of between £3,000 and £4,000. With 45 per cent of students earning less than £25,000 a year, the bursaries are critical to the college's access and retention policies. Birkbeck draws students from right across the capital, and with 64 per cent of the 2013 intake coming from ethnic minority groups, the issue of learning support is a priority. As Caroline said:

> Many of our students experience some kind of poverty – either social, cultural, or economic. The old term 'poverty' simply doesn't capture it any more.

Working during the day and attending college three or four evenings a week for three or four years is the life of a mature student at this extraordinary place. Those who come through the outreach programme face an even greater challenge, and it is a tribute to Caroline's team that the retention rate at the college remains so high. She claims that studying at Birkbeck is a liberating experience and one in line with George Birkbeck's original vision. The evidence is overwhelming.

Behind the impressive figures lie a wealth of extraordinary achievements by some very determined people. Nine Birkbeck students from the main Malet Street campus volunteered to write their stories and

I want to look at three of these in more detail. Those I have selected are broadly representative of the college's students across all subject areas. Gerald, the first of the Birkbeck students represented here, epitomizes all that is good about adult education and what Richard Hoggart described as 'the distinctive virtues of human beings'.

Figure 12: Birkbeck College student Gerald Nathanson stands proudly alongside his London cab. Like hundreds of others, Gerald combined a busy working life with studying for an evening degree at Birkbeck College. (By kind permission of Birkbeck College.)

EDUCATING GERALD

My name is Gerald Nathanson. I was always conscious of the fact that I did not have an education that would have given me a chance to achieve goals that demanded O and A levels. I attended 11 schools without passing exams, although I did well in woodwork, sports – swimming, boxing, gymnastics, 120-yard high hurdles, 440-yard obstacle race, fencing – and getting the cane.

Born in 1934, I was evacuated three times. All these movements precluded continuity of education, but I did pass practical exams in nursing as a medic in the Royal Air Force, Bomber Command. It was in 2008 that I said to my wife, Carole, and my sons that I would like to study for a BA at the Open University – without finishing the sentence they all said go for it. It was when I was one of the guests at a rotary club evening that I met Sue Jackson, now Prof. Sue Jackson. I told her that I had written to the OU for their curriculum. Sue advised me to apply to Birkbeck College where it would be more hands-on than the OU and would not be distance learning.

I attended Birkbeck College open evening at the Royal National Hotel. When it was my turn to be interviewed, I was asked why I wanted to study at Birkbeck. My answer was rather naive, as I said I wanted to prove that Richard III was the rightful King of England. Later, on my way home, I thought that I had made a fool of myself with my answer and it was BA good-bye before I had even started. However, I had been given an application form to fill in along with my CV. I think that my being a Blue Badge Guide, which was a two-year course of history, helped somewhat in my being accepted.

On Monday 17 March 2009 I passed my advanced driving exam at the age of 74 and the next day I was invited to attend an interview with Dr Hilary Sapire at Birkbeck. I knocked on her door and a voice said 'come in'. I placed one leg inside the door and said, 'Prof. Hilary, before I come in, have I been accepted?' With a smile she said, 'Come in Gerald and sit down.' In two days I had achieved two goals: one to prove that I could still drive properly and the other to be accepted into the University of London.

I bought myself a small pink notebook that had an elastic band round it, which showed how unprepared I was to study at college. My first lecture was an introduction to religion and the medieval life of Cathars and Catholics. Sitting beside me was a woman who, pointing her finger at my hearing aid, shouted at the lecturer, 'Speak up, this man is deaf.' I could have strangled her. At a reception later I was approached by one of the tutors who asked me how I enjoyed Prof. Innes's lecture. My answer was that I didn't understand a word of it. I also asked whether the lectures would always be like this in a room with 150 people. He reassured me that the most at a lecture would be 30. I was pleased, for as I listened to the conversations taking place I thought I was in another world. I was now having doubts. There were people in this room with degrees from Oxford and Cambridge universities. My thoughts went back to my 25-yard swimming certificate and how it did not compare to this august room of great minds.

Three weeks into my degree course, I had serious doubts as to my ability to stay at Birkbeck and made an appointment to see my designated tutor. The room was as I imagined it to be, with brown leather armchairs, wall-to-wall books. My tutor was tall in his grey, double-breasted suit and a mop of grey hair, not Michael Caine in *Educating Rita*. I told him that I had doubts about my future at the college and that I didn't know it was an honours course, again my naivety to the fore.

He explained that in his position as designated tutor he looked only to students with family and financial problems. I got up and walked out of his room and was prepared to call it a day. As luck would have it my seminar tutor was emerging from his own office just a few doors down the corridor, Lucas Balomenos. He asked me if I had any problems. I related to him my doubts about continuing with the course, to which he said, and I remember very clearly his words, 'If you need to talk to anyone come to me, because you are going to get your degree.' I cherished his words, and all at Birkbeck, tutors, librarians, and all the staff gave me the confidence to continue with the course.

I did not find it easy. It required extreme dedication and sacrifices. I studied on average eight hours a day, and read volumes of books and wrote many thousands of words. In four years at college I never missed a lecture and presented my essays and gave my presentations every term. Deadlines were kept and my fellow students comforted each other particularly in the bar after lectures. We were not drunk with drink, we were drunk with knowledge that we had absorbed through research and lectures.

The relief on completing a three-hour exam manifested itself in the college bar where, if the sun shone, we would gather on the terrace and indulge in a recap of the questions. To the relief of my family I managed to scrape through every exam culminating in my achieving a BA Hons. I loved every day of those four years – hard, yes, very hard, but it gave me a great sense of being somebody, somebody who has had a UNIVERSITY education, and Birkbeck gave me a new life.

Gerald speaks with passion, humour, and a refreshing honesty about his time at Birkbeck. His story takes us to the heart of what it means to be an adult studying at degree level. On the one hand the anxiety, almost fear, of walking into a tutorial for the first time, the ever-present doubt in your own ability, and the loss of confidence in the face of such a daunting challenge. On the other, the thrill of learning a new discipline, the excitement in passing difficult exams, the joy found in the camaraderie of other mature students, and the delight and pride, at last against all odds, in achieving your dream. As Gerald wrote, 'Birkbeck gave me a new life.'

Bridget Fuller's story is very different. Bridget grew up in a working-class agricultural community where education was 'not for the likes of us'. For a bright girl like Bridget this was incredibly frustrating. She tried hard at school, but was bullied for being a 'swot' and soon forgot any wild notions she might harbour of achieving a better life. As a result of her childhood experiences, which included serious medical problems, Bridget has 'felt a failure all my life', with a 'massive chip on my shoulder'. But with the help of counselling, she slowly overcame her childhood problems and began to rebuild her life. She took a job in a bookshop and, encouraged by her counsellor, enrolled on an access course and began to imagine the possibility of a degree. In her access course she discovered what was to become a passion. She fell in love with art history. Let Bridget pick up the story:

I AM A GRADUATE!

I can't remember how it came up. I suppose I was moaning to a friend about my lack of options. She told me about Birkbeck, which offered evening degree courses. I got in touch, got a prospectus. And there it was. I could study for a degree, in the subject I wanted, during the evening, at a place that was less than an hour away by train, at a college ten minutes from the station. I applied and was offered an interview. It was a terrifying experience and I was appalling! Incredibly bad. My lack of confidence and a belief that I don't really deserve good things to happen to me means the person I present to others is sometimes awkward, nervous, and really far, far away from the real me. But, unbelievably, I was offered a place to study for a degree in art history. I grabbed the opportunity, decided to take it one day at a time, and see what happened.

That was in 2007. Now in December 2013, I am still at Birkbeck, and beginning to think about my dissertation for the Masters degree I am studying. I am on a Renaissance studies course. After four years of studying art history, I was ready to move on to history proper, so to speak. It hasn't been plain sailing. My own history means that I have almost a phobic response to speaking out in class. This in fact was a major element in my belief that I would never be able to study for a degree. In the end I decided to carry on regardless and hope it wouldn't be too big a problem. It has been, but somehow I managed to get through in spite of it, though I wish I had been able to ask for help or at least make my tutors aware of it – until very recently.

I've almost forgotten the most important thing. I did of course get my degree. I thought I'd be happy with a 2.2, but was for a large part of the course straddling 2.2 and 2.1. Not the best place to be. The results came out and I was getting texts from friends telling me what they'd got and asking what my result was. I rushed to the internet to check to find that I had got ... a library fine!

I wasn't able to access my results until I'd paid the fine but the result finally appeared and I can never describe what it felt like to see 2.1 there. It was magical. I was and am so proud of myself. I am a graduate! I have a degree. I didn't want to leave Birkbeck and I wanted to carry on learning. A second degree is now possible. Getting back into education has been the best thing I've ever done.

The opportunity offered by Birkbeck has helped Bridget to overcome some deep-seated fears and anxieties. As she explains so eloquently, her academic ability has been allowed to flourish in the quiet corridors, libraries, and lectures halls of Birkbeck College, one of the world's most prestigious centres of adult higher education.

If Bridget and Gerald arrived at Birkbeck from very different directions, our third student illustrates the value of the college in changing the lives of people for the better. Mustapha Gedhalraby Sow arrived in London from his native Sierra Leone in 2006. There were few opportunities in Sierra Leone for an ambitious, intelligent young person like Mustapha to study at HE level. He knew he needed to study for a degree in order to pursue his aim of becoming a journalist, so he left his family and friends to follow his dream. Mustapha was shocked to find so many opportunities for people of all ages to study for a degree in the UK. He quickly found a job and then registered for a BA in journalism and media at Birkbeck.

GIVING PEOPLE A CHANCE

When I arrived in England there were many opportunities to study, even at my age. And seeing people of all ages studying was what actually inspired me and gave me a phenomenal impetus to do the same and proceed as far as I could. I chose the wonderful Birkbeck College, University of London, which gave me the opportunity to both work and study in the evening.

My aspirations for the future had always been one thing – to do all in my capability to achieve my dream of being a journalist. My studying at this high level has had a profound effect on me, in terms of personal development. It has given me added confidence in whatever I am doing, changing my perception of many things. With the education I now have the power of thinking, and analysing things critically has led me to believe that certain things I perceived as great were actually not and that certain things I overlooked, due to ignorance, were some of the most important things in life. My education has given me the drive to perform extremely well in any vocation, also being overly conscientious when executing any duties that I am expected to perform, thanks to the enormous amount of skills that I have acquired from studying at Birkbeck.

I am now a highly regarded coach both for South West Trains (Metro Area) and the Rail, Maritime & Transport Union. I represent staff in many different meetings involving senior management – something which is definitely the result of management deeming necessary for me to pursue such roles not only due to my education, but most importantly because of the way I utilize it to ensure I always do an efficient job. I can authoritatively say that I now command massive respect among my colleagues, but most importantly within management circles. I have even had a secondment in the company's internal communications department which would been a mere dream a few years ago. My knowledge of the English language has improved and I am now more than capable of handling any kind of writing or communication in the language almost flawlessly with the enormous amount of confidence Birkbeck has instilled in me.

I would argue that the wisest thing I have done for myself is coming to England. I would never have attained this level of education at my age, in my beloved Sierra Leone. This is not to say I did not get a good educational base in my country, one that enabled me to cope with the challenges I faced when I started my undergraduate course. I was lucky to attend the best and most prestigious schools in Sierra Leone – The Holy Trinity Boys Primary School and the Prince of Wales School in the capital city, Freetown. In my country it has always been 'education for sale', which simply means that you have to have the means to pay for your education. If you cannot afford to pay, that might just be the end of the road.

I would conclude this story by saying that I will, without any doubt, return to my beloved Sierra Leone, take back what I have gained from my education in England and make proper use of it by helping my compatriots gain what I have gained, by campaigning for the right to education for everyone, regardless of age. My message to my old country would be – give people a chance to make use of their lives through education at any point they may want to in their lives, it works!

Mustapha has joint Sierre Leone and British citizenship and received a warm welcome at Birkbeck. His plea to his country is profound – give people hope. Like Gerald and Bridget he showed tremendous determination in completing his degree. At 75 years old, Gerald is retired, while Bridget and Mustapha both have demanding full-time jobs. The educational experience of all three students has been very different, but they share a tremendous passion for learning that Birkbeck College has nurtured and nourished. They are three very special students and they, like hundreds of others at this exceptional place, owe their opportunity to George Birkbeck and the working men who crowded into the Crown and Anchor pub that damp and foggy December evening in 1823. To paraphrase the brilliant novelist, Nobel prize-winner, and chronicler of racial apartheid Nadine Gordimer, 'The past at Birkbeck College remains firmly in the present.'

From humble origins

From Paddington Station take the train to Oxford and leave the metropolitan hustle and bustle of Bloomsbury far behind. Within the hour you arrive at the ancient university town. A ten-minute stroll through the town takes you past the cloistered calm of twelfth-century Balliol College and, on your right, the imposing presence of the Radcliffe Camera and the Bodleian Library. At the end of Holywell Street turn left into Mansfield Road and you will find the smallest, but one of the most interesting colleges of Oxford University. The rather awkwardly named Harris Manchester College (HMC) is a full member college of the university but admits only students over the age of 21, who study for full Oxford degrees and postgraduate programmes.

Originally administered by Presbyterians, HMC was one of a handful of dissenting academies that provided higher education from the late eighteenth century. Oxford and Cambridge universities were, of course, staunchly Anglican. Radical theology has been at the core of teaching and learning throughout the college's history, along with more modern subjects such as science, modern languages, and history. One of the key people in the history of the college was Charles Wellbeloved, a Unitarian minister. Wellbeloved was adamant that the school should not be called Unitarian because he wanted students to have an open mind and to discover religious and spiritual truth for themselves. In 1809 he wrote to George Wood:

> I do not and will not teach Unitarianism or any ism but Christianism. I will endeavour to teach the students how to study the Scripture ... nice if they find Unitarianism there ... only let them find something for themselves.
>
> (Wellbeloved, 1809: letter to a friend)

This is consistent with a motto in the college chapel window, '*Elargissez Dieu*', broadly translated as 'Set God free' or 'Broaden your conception of God'. Despite this liberal approach to teaching religion, the majority of the early students were Unitarian and the college continues to stage Unitarian worship on a regular basis. However, HMC is no longer dominated by religious thinking, but continues the liberal strand of its tradition by providing second-chance opportunities to mature students. Small by Oxford standards, the college draws students from around the world, making studying at HMC a truly international experience. Despite its modest size, the students are fortunate to enjoy one of the largest libraries in the university. Built by Sir Henry Tate, sugar baron and benefactor of the Tate Gallery, the library is an enchanting retreat for those seeking quiet contemplation and the intellectual fellowship many of them crave. How those library lovers we met in Chapter 1, Jack Stevens and Malcolm Williams, would have cherished the opportunity to have spent time in the quiet splendour of the library at Harris Manchester College.

Figure 13: Harris Manchester College from Holywell Street in the centre of Oxford, minutes from the Bodleian Library. The William Morris-inspired stained-glass windows are a feature of the architecture of this delightful building. (By kind permission of HMC.)

Another jewel in the HMC crown is its delightful chapel. On a visit to the college in Spring 2013, I was fortunate to be escorted around one of the most beautiful buildings in Oxford. The college chapel is a Pre-Raphaelite jewel with breathtaking stained-glass windows designed by Edward Burne-Jones and crafted by William Morris. According to Pevsner's *Buildings of England–Oxfordshire*, the whole set of Burne-Jones windows in Manchester College Chapel of 1893–8 is 'a pure joy'. With architectural gems like the library and the chapel, it is little wonder that HMC students speak so highly of their college. Perhaps the most interesting questions regarding HMC students are what inspired them to undertake a residential Oxford degree and what happens to them after they graduate? The answer to these questions should reveal how much HMC has adapted to the modern world since its inception in the late eighteenth century.

Together, eight Harris Manchester students participated in the research for this book, three of whom wrote extended pieces about their education and their time at the college. Before we look at the student experience, it is worth considering the qualities required of adults studying at this elevated level. Sustained critical engagement with their subject is near the top of the list. Determination and a capacity for hard work, intellectual curiosity, and imagination, of either a literary, historical, or scientific kind, are all prerequisites of studying at Birkbeck and HMC. Sandra Valdini, Andrew Brown, and Angie Johnson possess these qualities in abundance. We will see that not all of our adult students find immediate success at the end of their studies. Many take years to adjust to their new life. Sandra Valdini found her way to HMC from Germany, where she spent the early part of her life.

Nurse, sculptor, and scholar

In my early 20s I wanted to be a sculptor like my uncle. My uncle was a very talented sculptor. I loved to draw since I was little, and later I started making small sculptures out of soapstone. After oiling and polishing the stone, looking at this beautiful little woman that I had just created, I felt a new sense of pride and accomplishment.

At the time I made this sculpture I was stuck in a job that I didn't really like. Being a nurse was tough. Although I had left school at 16, it took me almost two years to get a training place, mainly owing to my poor grades and unconvincing performance at job interviews. But eventually I was accepted at a nursing school in Laupheim, southern Germany. The work soon took a toll on my physical and mental health. Nevertheless, after three years I graduated. I quickly managed to find work at the teaching hospital of Ulm University, situated halfway between Stuttgart to the north-west and Munich to the north-east.

In 2001 I finally decided to make my passion my profession and become a stonemason's apprentice. I submitted 40 applications and received 39 rejections and one offer for an internship place. During this short week of my internship I felt, for the first time, that I was doing what I was meant to do. While I managed to convince the shop's junior manager that I was good enough, he informed me that his father had decided to go with the more traditional choice and hire a male apprentice instead of me.

I knew that I didn't want to keep working as a nurse, but I was running out of alternatives. So I asked my father, also a stonemason, if he could take me on as his apprentice. But dad was having none of it and said I should return to school and get my Abitur, the German equivalent of A levels, and then go on to study at university. At first I was angry. I saw myself as a manual worker and artist rather than an academic.

So in the autumn of 2003 I enrolled at Night School Ulm. I didn't expect to do too well, mainly because I was convinced that I wasn't really book smart. Also, in order to sustain myself financially over the next three years I had to continue working part time as a nurse, which would limit the time for homework and revision. Nevertheless, I did much better than I had hoped. I excelled at every subject I studied, eagerly absorbing every new piece of information I was given. It was at night school that I experienced something that could be best described as a sense of accomplishment and pride at being the top at something I didn't even expect to be average at. I studied and revised tirelessly until there was little else in my life than work and study. By the time my second year at night school came to a close I knew what I wanted to do after my Abitur: go to university!

Over the last 26 years I had grown tired of Germany and wanted to start a new life and what better way of finding a good job in England than to graduate from an English university. The first time I actually went to England was only after I had been offered a place at Oxford. I decided to use my last application for Cambridge or Oxford, not because I expected to be successful, but I didn't want to waste that final application. I finally picked Oxford and chose philosophy, politics, and economics as my subjects.

Universities like Oxford and Cambridge are, even now, still viewed by many as socially exclusive. While I did encounter some elitist behaviour as a student, there certainly was no such bias in the selection process. I don't remember much of the interviews, other than my struggle to make myself understood in coherent English. It seemed more important to the tutors to see how well I managed to apply my general understanding of philosophy, politics, and economics to solve a given problem. If I remember correctly, my politics tutor started by giving me a text by John Stuart Mill on plural voting to read before asking me to analyse and offer criticism of the text.

My philosophy tutor asked me to give him a definition of 'bad'. It seemed to me that, whatever my tutors were looking for in a student went beyond the ability to answer questions 'correctly' or make the 'right' impression. Instead, creativity in problem-solving and passion for the subject appeared to matter more to my future tutors than the school I attended or how eloquent my English was. About two weeks after the interviews I received my letter offering me a place to study philosophy, politics, and economics at Harris Manchester College, University of Oxford. This surprising news gave me a confidence boost in my Abitur finals, and I achieved the highest grades at Night School Ulm since its foundation.

At Oxford, most people are at least as smart as you and at least as good as you. I did not meet a single student who wasn't extraordinarily intelligent, at least when it came to the subject they studied. When I started studying at Oxford, I felt that I had two disadvantages. First, the level of the subjects I studied at night school was insufficient to prepare me for the great challenge of studying three different subjects at a place like Oxford. The second disadvantage, which was far more noticeable in philosophy than in economics, was my lack of English speaking and writing skills. But what more than made up for these disadvantages was my ability to work hard, harder than many of my fellow students.

I graduated with a 2.1 in the midst of the worst economic crisis since the Great Depression. I am not sure if I should continue at this point, as the story of my astonishing journey to Oxford is over, and what little inspiration it may have offered to its readers will probably be lost if I continue. Still, my life went on after graduating from Oxford, albeit not in the way that I had imagined.

I didn't manage to find a job, so after graduation I moved back into my parents' home in Germany. After a few months of unsuccessful applications I felt my dream of living and working abroad was slipping away, and so I decided to take the next flight to the one place that was bound to offer a job for a hard-working immigrant: London. I managed to find a tiny, but cheap room in east London and a job as a night receptionist at a hotel on Trafalgar Square. After a year, I managed to get promotion to the position of income auditor at the famous Waldorf Hotel. My year at the Waldorf was a great one, even though I eventually decided to leave London and return to Oxford.

I decided to return to Oxford for two main reasons: career progression and nostalgia. I accepted a job working for the university as a student financial support assistant. But as well as helping students overcome their financial hardship, I spent a lot of time copying papers and posting letters. After a year of copying and posting, I took up my current job. The job of gift registry assistant is a data-entry job, and while the work itself is not very taxing, the past year has been very difficult. This was partly because of my great disappointment at having yet again ended up in a dead-end job, which in turn didn't make me the easiest colleague to get along with. I started an accounting qualification, ACCA, in 2013. I passed my first exams, but I'm not really convinced that I have made the right choice.

As I am writing this final paragraph, 2013 is almost over. While I feel somehow stuck since my return to Oxford, I still hope that some day I will find whatever it is that will reignite the passion and happiness I felt during that short week as a stonemason's intern. I have recently started drawing again, but I'm a bit rusty, and my hands are not yet able to do what they could some 12 years ago. We'll see.

Like Hardy's Jude, Sandra harboured dreams of becoming a stonemason; unlike Jude, Sandra actually realized her dream of a place at Oxford University. Her story has some chapters left to run and her quiet determination will ensure she achieves her goals. Her story, written with honesty and passion, reveals much about the dreams, ambitions, and life of a mature student determined to change her life.

Like many of the adults I met during the course of the research, as a youngster Angie Johnson attended a secondary modern school. In her 20s she took A levels as a mature student with dreams of studying for a degree. Within a couple of years, and to her great shock, Angie found herself at in the city of 'dreaming spires' studying for a degree. Now with an MA, Angie takes great pleasure watching her own daughters follow in her academic footsteps.

THREE OF THE HAPPIEST YEARS OF MY LIFE

When my daughters were born I worried they would fulfil ambitions that I hadn't got round to doing myself. I went to a secondary modern school where we were not expected to achieve much academically and was actively discouraged from doing so. So I went back into education to take my A levels.

I started with English at the local adult education centre. After enjoying the first year so much I decided to add history to my programme. I wanted to do the Renaissance period, but this was being taught only at the local comprehensive – so I asked if they would let me take part. They agreed, thinking it would be a good experiment to have adult students in with their sixth formers. It was a beneficial experience for all of us I believe.

My results turned out pretty good. I had read that a major contributory factor to youngsters thriving academically was if their parent had a degree. I decided I would apply for university. I applied to my local universities – who both offered me a place. But as there was a spare place on the UCAS form my (now ex) husband dared me to put down Oxford. So I did and was gobsmacked to be offered an interview at Harris Manchester. I knew right away that it was the right place for me but was astonished that they felt the same way and offered me a place.

Then followed three of the happiest years of my life. The support from the college was terrific. For example, families were all invited into hall for Sunday lunch. In half-term school holidays my tutor let the girls come in while I had my tutorials and my fellow students all had real-life things to juggle, just like me. My daughters benefited so much from the experience; they saw that learning was fun and not something to be intimidated by, and that nothing was out of reach if you were prepared to work hard for it.

I went on to do a Masters in playwriting studies at the University of Birmingham, a prestigious course where I met and worked with many of the leading practitioners in the theatre today. Following that I worked as a writer/producer and also as press officer for a large theatre. I still write plays and I am now a theatre reviewer. In addition, I work for the university. Because the theatre pays so badly I would not be able to support my daughters through the Masters courses they are now on. I am still close to HMC and am grateful beyond words for what they have done for me.

Angie's is a life-affirming story and encapsulates what is possible for a determined mature student with an irresistible yearning to change his or her situation. Harris Manchester College provided the opportunity and Angie took full advantage. One of the most interesting consequences of Angie's academic journey is the way it has inspired her daughters, and Angie is fully aware of this. Her old secondary school must seem a very long way away.

Our final HMC student is the Revd Andrew Brown. Oxford changed Andrew Brown's life in the most profound manner. His was by some way the longest story I received from all the participants. As hard as I tried, I found it extremely difficult to cut. With Andrew's agreement here is an edited version of his remarkable story:

WHAT IS THIS LIFE?

What is this life if, full of care,
We have no time to stand and stare.

No time to turn at Beauty's glance,
And watch her feet, how they can dance.

A poor life this if, full of care,
We have no time to stand and stare.

('Leisure' by William Henry Davies,
stanzas 1, 5 and 7 Songs of Joy and Others)

Returning to formal university study at Harris Manchester College, Oxford, in 1997 as a 33-year-old adult was one of the most surprising but also exciting, exacting, and creative moments of my life. For the experience I remain hugely grateful, both to the University of Oxford, to the General Assembly of Unitarian and Free Christian Churches, and to my wife, Susanna, for selflessly supporting and encouraging me throughout those three, challenging, years.

I always struggled with the formal, classroom-based education I experienced during the 1980s at Tendring High School in Essex. I think the reason for this was that in every other learning context I was never taught fact 'x', simply to move on as quickly as possible to fact 'y' and 'z' in order to pass some official examination. Instead, I was always allowed to linger with 'x' and to play with it at length before moving on. The two key examples of this way of learning were had by me in poetry and music.

Thanks to my paternal grandmother and my English teacher at school, Mrs Hill, reading and thinking about poetry early on became part of my everyday life. As will become apparent, introductions to Khayyam and Housman were to prove, many years later, key to helping me to enter fully into the Oxford learning experience.

As a teenager I took to scouring the local second-hand bookshops for poetry I liked and, very early on, I stumbled across many of the poets involved in the San Francisco renaissance of the late 1940s and 1950s. At the time I was particularly drawn to the work of Robert Creeley. I discovered that his short poems were the perfect texts to have tucked into my jacket pocket ready for those quiet moments when, during a rest on a long walk or cycle ride out into the rural Essex coastal landscape, I found myself lying on my back on the grass with time to think long and hard about life. This showed me how staying with a poem for a whole day often allowed an astonishing range of interpretations to emerge, which, in turn, were able to provoke me to think about the poem and to see the world in many different ways. It is perhaps no surprise that, slowly, this made me want to try my own hand at philosophizing and writing. But poetry and thinking were not my only schoolboy passions – there was also music.

Since childhood I'd gone to the local church and was a member of the choir and also a bell-ringer, so I had had a pretty good introduction to the basics of music. Then, aged 14, while staying near Munich with a German family on an exchange visit, I was fully immersed in the favourite music of my hosts – that of the Beatles and the Beach Boys – and I came back to the UK desperate to join a band. There was someone in my class, Mark Sainsbury, who already played the guitar and loved the Beatles and he persuaded me to try the instrument played by both Paul McCartney and Brian Wilson – the bass guitar. After more than a little persuasion, my parents eventually agreed to get me one for my 15th birthday. Now my grandmother heard about this and she was very keen that I should also have some way to get involved in classical music, which she loved. She discovered that the equivalent classical instrument to a bass guitar was the double bass and so, to my surprise, on my 15th birthday I found in the sitting room both a bass guitar and a double bass. It was a memorable, life-changing day.

Now, I grew up in a small, rural coastal village in Essex and there were simply no bass teachers nearby and so the only way to begin to learn how to play these instruments was to listen, over and over again, to the records I loved and to try to copy what I heard. For the bass guitar the choice of records to copy was easy – those by the Beatles and the Beach Boys. But for the double bass the choice of what to copy wasn't so obvious – playing along by ear to Beethoven's symphonies didn't appeal, even though, for my grandmother's sake, I tried. So, instead, I went through my parents' small record collection and was lucky to find Dave Brubeck's two most famous albums, *Time Out* and *Time Further Out*. I immediately fell in love with them and so, along with my Beatles and Beach Boys records, I stayed with them for months and months and, quite literally, played along with them. Slowly but surely, how rock, pop, and jazz music worked gradually began to make sense to me.

This burgeoning love of music and poetry meant, of course, that I spent all the time I should have been preparing for my O and then A levels in reading my newly discovered poets and figuring out how to play rock and roll and jazz bass. In the formal, academic school environment this proved to be a disaster. I got indifferent O level grades and, for my A levels (in English and History), two highly undistinguished E grades.

Not surprisingly, neither my teachers nor my parents were best pleased with this and, together, they decided that on finishing school I had to get a job, immediately. I was gently, but very firmly, encouraged to apply for jobs in either a local bank or insurance brokers. This thought filled me with horror and it encouraged me to scour the local newspaper job columns for other, more attractive options. I could not believe my eyes when I saw an advert for a sales assistant's post in a local poetry bookshop attached to Colchester Arts Centre and I lost no time in getting my application to them.

A few days later I was offered an interview and duly presented myself at the bookshop. I was greeted by a man who was to prove pivotal in my education, John Row. John was himself a poet who had been part of the British Beat movement. With his long white hair, John Lennon-like glasses and general beatnik demeanour, he looked very much like the kind of person I thought it would be great to work with. My interview was simple and startling. There were a few of the usual introductory questions after which I told him about my love of jazz and poetry, especially that of Robert Creeley and the Beat movement in general. His reply was to lean over to one of the shelves, pull out a copy of Allen Ginsberg's seminal poem 'Howl' and begin to read. I was amazed and utterly captivated. When he finished, he looked up and asked me what I thought of that? I replied, 'Fucking amazing!' He beamed, and said, 'OK, you've got the job.'

Immediately picking up on the fact that I liked Creeley's work, John lent me a book by Martin Duberman called *Black Mountain: An exploration in community* (Dutton, 1972) about the extraordinary liberal arts school called Black Mountain College, which operated in North Carolina between 1933 and 1957. Creeley had been a member of its faculty. Here is not the place to explore the history and ethos of the college but it encouraged the kind of education that I already knew I found particularly congenial. At Black Mountain College, students were able to linger, creatively, over their subjects and they could, and would, meet people across the entire artistic spectrum in both the classroom and in various social settings. I was captivated by what I read and assiduously began to learn about the work of its teachers in an attempt to experience, if only at second-hand, something of the education Black Mountain College had offered its students. In music I followed up the work of John Cage, Lou Harrison, and Stefan Wolpe; in poetry I continued to read Robert Creeley but added the work of Charles Olson; in architecture I looked into the extraordinary world of Buckminster Fuller and, in the world of painting, I sought out works by Willem de Kooning and Franz Kline. I lingered long over the work of them all and all of it continues to inform and enrich my life.

The three years I spent in John's bookshop following up my newfound leads were extraordinary. Not only was I able to read countless books of poetry and essays but, because the shop was attached to an arts centre, I also got to meet and hear dozens of contemporary poets and attend many jazz concerts. It was only natural that while there I finally began to write myself and also to pick up a few jazz gigs. I could barely believe my luck. Perhaps the high point of that period was getting the opportunity to play with the great jazz guitarist Tal Fallow, who had played with Charlie Parker and one of my own bass heroes, Charlie Mingus.

But John Row was also a performer himself, and so I did a great many jazz and poetry gigs with him at various arts and music festivals around East Anglia – often in a band called John Row's Sound Proposition. Driving back very, very late from one of them, John and I passed close by the village of Little Gidding, which had inspired T.S. Eliot to write one of the poems in his *Four Quartets*. I persuaded John that it would be well worth stopping at the village church to see the dawn break. He agreed. During our conversation, while we waited for the sun to rise, I said to him that I deeply regretted not being able to have had a Black Mountain education myself. Very slowly he turned towards me and said, 'And what do you think I've been giving you for the last three years?' Just as the sun rose over Little Gidding another kind of dawn broke in my head as I realized this was exactly what had happened. I take that dawn to have been the graduation ceremony from my first real university course – a course which, had I not taken and completed, I would not have been able either to get into, or to get so much from, Oxford University. Just like Khayyam and Housman, Little Gidding was to play an important part in helping me to make the most of my Oxford experience.

From that dawn onwards I began to enter fully into a career as a jazz and rock musician, playing, touring, and recording with all kinds of people, even spending a while with Steve Harley in his band Cockney Rebel. However, during this time I never stopped reading and thinking. Over the years reading all that poetry had encouraged me to begin to ask, and think through, some of the perennial theological and philosophical questions and in consequence, I had also started to read widely in this field.

All through this period I had also remained actively involved with liberal churches. Religion had always been an interest of mine and during 1990–1 I properly explored whether or not I should become an Anglican priest. In the end my unconventional education and bohemian attitudes and lifestyle meant that I needed to be involved in a rather more open, non-conformist community. Luck was on my side. In the nearest large town to where Susanna and I were living, we discovered just such a radical tradition at the Ipswich Unitarian Meeting House. It was the ideal place for me to think creatively through the 'big questions' of life and, while there, the call to ministry became increasingly insistent.

Eventually, I gave in to it and formally applied for ministerial training. In 1996, my application was accepted. Now the two places one can train for the Unitarian and Free Christian ministry are at the Unitarian College, Manchester, and at what is today one of Britain's foremost mature student societies, Harris Manchester College, Oxford. This college was, initially, a Unitarian foundation, being the direct descendent of the dissenting Warrington Academy, which was active between 1756 and 1782. For all kinds of practical reasons – not least of all because it was nearer to Suffolk where Susanna and I were living – I expressed a preference for Oxford and an interview for the Oxford, Bachelor of Theology (BTh) was duly arranged.

I was extremely nervous about this. After all, two dodgy A levels at E grade were far from being trump cards. However, the surprises began immediately. My interviews with the principal, the Revd Dr Ralph Waller, and then the Senior tutor, Dr (now Professor) Lesley Smith, were more akin to the free-flowing, open-ended, creative conversations on the subject I was used to having with people during my 'Black-Mountainesque' education with John Row. It also became apparent that my odd educational story, far from being a black mark against me, was taken as a positive indication that I might prove to be an ideal mature student. I noticed I wasn't particularly being asked about how many 'book facts' I knew about theology but was, instead, primarily being encouraged to show whether I could do something interesting and creative with what I already knew. In short, those two interviews made me feel that, educationally speaking, I might just have found some kind of institutional, educational home. To my delight and surprise, a few days later I was offered a place starting in the Michaelmas term of October 1997.

The second homecoming experience was had in the very first formal class of my first term. It was an Old Testament class with Father John Davies and the subject was wisdom literature, beginning with the book of Ecclesiastes. I knew the basic stories and content of most books in the Bible simply because of my church upbringing but, as yet, I had engaged in no formal, critical study of the texts. Again I was very nervous. Perhaps my interview experience had simply been an anomaly and now I was about to encounter the brutal truth that I was not up to an Oxford education.

But there then occurred what remains one of the most surprising moments of my life. Father John began the class, not as I expected, by referring in any shape or form to the Old Testament but by closing his eyes, leaning back in his chair and reciting, from memory, a dozen or so verses from *The Rubaiyat of Omar Khayyam* and a couple of poems from Housman's *A Shropshire Lad*. I could barely believe what I had just heard! Fr John opened his eyes, leaned forward on to the desk and began to show us how the themes of these poems resonated with the major themes of the book of Ecclesiastes. The first week's reading list he gave us included not only Ecclesiastes, but also these two collections of poems. The essay question he set encouraged us to use these poems to help us get to grips with what the authors of the biblical text might have been trying to say. Long ago these poems had become very much my own and so I found myself entering, almost seamlessly, into what would otherwise have been the unfamiliar worlds of an Oxford University seminar and third-century BCE Hebrew thought. As I walked out of that class into the warm October sun of 1997 to walk back to college across Magdalen Bridge I felt quite ecstatic.

The third important homecoming experience of my first term occurred after a number of tutorials with Sister Benedicta Ward on the subject of Christian spirituality. For my essay on this course I asked her whether I could undertake a study of the seventeenth-century religious community of Little Gidding under the leadership of Nicholas Ferrar (1592–1637). I had told Sr Benedicta about my earlier experience there and an essay on the community's activity seemed to fit the course requirements perfectly. She agreed and arranged for me to visit the library of St John's College, which held a number of original documents from the community.

The opportunity to access such rare source material is unusual for undergraduates but, being that much older than the usual undergraduate, and having a reference from Sr Benedicta, I found the doors of the library opened up to me. The moment I picked up those unique documents and turned their pages with my own hands in order to do a piece of serious research, I suddenly felt like a real scholar. I remember stopping reading and suddenly realizing I was truly *here* and that, for all my rebellious non-conformity, educationally speaking, I was where I belonged. I sat there for a long, long time taking it all in. I felt that this was the moment when I knew my 'needle' had properly clicked into the Oxford 'groove'.

Of course, none of this meant that everything was always joyously easy and a complete bundle of laughs. The significant practical difficulty I faced was the need to develop quickly the discipline and skill of writing two academic essays a week for my tutorials. Learning this skill was often exhausting and deeply frustrating. Like many others, I had dozens of anxious and sleepless nights worrying about whether I could really pull this off. Fortunately, I could see that this was a vital skill for a minister to develop (as they are required to write a new address almost every week of the year) and this provided me with enough energy and enthusiasm not to give up.

Even on the most difficult days, what continued to thrill me during my time at HMC was the opportunity to spend a whole week reading about and reflecting upon just one or two subjects. Just as I had found it so rewarding in earlier years to lie on my back in the grass and think long and hard about a single poem, I found it equally rewarding to do the same with theological/philosophical texts. I quickly discovered that simply sitting at my desk in my room or in some library, even one as grand as the Bodleian, just didn't work for me and that every essay I wrote without taking a long reflective walk was always the worse for it. The need for 'time to stand and stare' I had learned on the Essex coast was deeply reaffirmed during my time at Oxford. Indeed, in my third year, while studying philosophy of religion, I was delighted that my tutor, Prof. Victor Nuovo, agreed with me that some part of our tutorials would be better spent walking out of doors.

Another thing that continued to inspire me during my studies was the realization that I experienced almost no social or class discrimination at all. As a state school lad from an aspirant working-class family, the possibility of this had caused me some concern before 'going up'. There were, of course, certain aspects of Oxford to do with class and social privilege that I found deeply problematic, but the overriding impression I experienced was one of radical inclusivity. I remain profoundly impressed by this, often unacknowledged, fact.

Outside the immediate confines of Harris Manchester College I was always mixing with many undergraduates of the usual age and many of them were very interesting and delightful. However, I admit that I found the varied company of adult learners at HMC far more congenial and rewarding. I experienced this most powerfully at the college dinner table and in its junior common room. Like most people, I quickly found out that I was going to learn at least as much from these social encounters as I was ever going to learn from my books, tutorials, and classes. My former Black-Mountainesque education meant that I found this aspect of college life particularly exhilarating and I rarely left the dining hall without my head buzzing excitedly with some new idea or thought.

It was during those many conversations that I became fully aware that, for nearly all of us returning to education as adults, this time at Oxford really counted. It became apparent that we were all taking some kind of calculated risk to achieve here some kind of new opening in our lives. This exciting, heady, difficult, and risky undertaking naturally created a deep sense of camaraderie between us and the key friendships I formed in college during this time remain alive, vibrant, and sustaining even 14 years after my graduation.

And then, suddenly, it was all over. In August 2000, only two months after my final examinations, I found myself starting a new and very busy life as the minister of the Memorial (Unitarian) Church in Cambridge, the post I hold today. The knowledge, skills, and disciplines I learned at Oxford stood me in good stead for this job and it would not have been possible for me to work effectively in the Cambridge environment without my HMC education. What I learned in my early years helped me see something wonderful, if apparently paradoxical, about the Oxford educational system that I think I would otherwise have missed. It is something I would very much like to pass on to anyone thinking of giving it a go themselves.

The paradox of Oxford for me was discovered when I realized it was offering me a crash course in how I might better take time to stand and stare. Nearly all of us who come back to college as adults are being driven by some real or perceived need to 'prove ourselves' and to do well. Very few of us want to waste a moment of our time and it is very tempting to think that to get the most from our period at Oxford we must fill every moment of every hour with work, work, and more work. When you add all these factors together the subjective experience of an adult learner can be one in which there is absolutely no time to stand and stare. However, at Oxford, it quickly becomes apparent to most students that, even if they were able to fill every waking moment with the work of acquiring knowledge, they would still not be able to read every book on their subject, nor were they going to be able to write some final, absolute word on it. As the author of Ecclesiastes said, we all quickly learned that 'of making many books there is no end; and much study is a weariness of the flesh'.

Almost immediately after finishing college I received a delightful farewell birthday postcard from one of my fellow students who, I feel sure, always understood the importance of quiet and having time. It carried a picture of a stained-glass window in St Mary's, Winchester, depicting Izaak Walton fishing. The caption on the window contains words from I Thessalonians 4:11, which read, 'study to be quiet'. I feel that these words still best sum up not only what I learned during my childhood and first wonderful, eccentric educational experience with John Row, but also what I learned in my return to education as an adult. Of course, I do not always succeed in putting this very hard but important lesson into practice, but I continue to try and I draw a great deal of hope from some words found in Samuel Beckett's novella, *Worstward Ho*:

> All of old. Nothing else ever. Ever tried. Ever failed. No matter. Try again. Fail again. Fail better.

In writing this piece I became acutely aware of how my unusual education and the personal philosophy it has allowed me to develop has continued to mirror the beautiful, liminal, 'in-between' physical landscape in which I grew up. The Essex coastal village of Kirby-le-Soken with its complex network of creeks, mudflats, salt marsh, and big East Anglian sky is a landscape that cannot easily be categorized as being either fully earth, sea, or sky. I am struck by the fact that the Cambridgeshire Fens in the midst of which I now live and work are strikingly similar. Let me explain what I mean.

Standing in the midst of that Essex landscape was the parish church of St Michael's, where I became a faithful choirboy and bell-ringer. Within its walls I imbibed deeply the stories and prayers, music and hymns of a very English kind of Christianity. From my choir stall I had a clear sight of a very unusual east window. It did not show the crucifixion but rather three touching scenes from the life of Jesus as he engaged compassionately with three women. The window told a *human* story that contrasted strikingly with the complex, otherworldly, metaphysical claims concerning original sin, crucifixion, resurrection, redemption, and salvation that I heard preached from the pulpit. Pondering this each week in my choir stall I eventually came to affirm a completely naturalistic understanding of Jesus and the Christian tradition and, like Housman, I discovered that my picture of the universe had begun to look and feel more like that expressed by his own classical hero, the Roman poet and follower of Epicurus, Lucretius, whose sublime poem 'On the Nature of Things' expresses the transient joys and wonders of a completely natural universe in which our redemption as mortal beings is not from the world, but one found in it. Since that time, along with Housman's poetry, both Lucretius's poem and Epicurus's philosophy became as important to me as the gospels and their stories about the human Jesus.

Beneath Oxford's dreaming spires I was given an extraordinary opportunity to work out both how I might begin to inhabit and live creatively in that liminal, religious place that lay somewhere in between the Christianity of my childhood and the exciting, sceptical, materialistic philosophies of Greece and Rome I encountered in my teens, and also how to integrate the freedom of thought found in my earlier, informal education with the more formal and structured academic ways of Oxford.

At Oxford, thanks particularly to Victor Nuovo and Father John, I was able to do this, first through studying the liminal, 'in between' philosophies of Benedict Spinoza and the author of Ecclesiastes, and then, as I was leaving the city for that other place in the Fens, by beginning an exploration of the work of Nietzsche, Heidegger, Wittgenstein, and Ernst Bloch. My encounter with these post-Christian and post-metaphysical thinkers allowed me slowly to see that the disappearance of my belief in a monotheistic God, rather than being a disaster, had actually opened up what felt to me more relevant, contemporary ways to understand creation, and to encounter and talk about what we call the divine, the holy, and the sacred. This is, of course, itself a very liminal, 'in between', kind of religious faith – neither 'Christian' nor 'atheist' – but it at least has the benefit of being my own and one that I can fully hold with a clean heart.

Andrew's story needed telling in full. Most of our student stories are ones of redemption or self-fulfilment. Andrew's story lies somewhere between the two. HMC gave him the opportunity to develop both educationally and spiritually, while his music helped him to form his own holistic picture of the world. Andrew's account is exceptional in this respect. His time at HMC provided answers to many outstanding questions in his life and provides a deep insight to the experience of HMC students. Oxford gave him the time and guidance he needed to achieve the very peak of his intellectual and spiritual quest. Talented jazz musician, philosopher, and spiritual leader Andrew made the very best of his time at Oxford.

It is difficult to frame the stories of our three HMC students within tightly constructed social and political theories. We can see from the experience of Sandra, Angie, and Andrew that adult students defy such convenient categories. Social justice is less of a priority for Harris Manchester College than it is for our other adult centres. HMC is about providing adults with the highest possible standard of undergraduate and postgraduate study. Entry requirements are rigorous. One of our group reported being asked for A level grades of AAB to allow him to follow his passion for history. At Birkbeck College and the Open University there are no formal entry requirements, although standards at both institutions are extremely challenging. All members of our Harris Manchester group attended state schools where, for one reason or another, their potential was either overlooked or crushed. Stereotypical family and social attitudes held back the female members of the group, before they found their voice in their 20s or 30s. HMC has not only continued to provide a higher education in the spirit of its founders at Warrington back in 1757, but has also established what Andrew Brown referred to in his story as a 'radical inclusivity'. Our Oxford student stories illustrate how the HMC has retained its original aims, while adapting successfully to the needs of mature students over 250 years later. It is a remarkable institution and a vital component of adult learning in the UK.

Chapter 6

All thanks to the OU

> What other nation in the world could have given us William Shakespeare, pork pies, Christopher Wren, Windsor Great Park, the Open University, *Gardeners' Question Time* and the chocolate digestive biscuit?
>
> (Bill Bryson, author and honorary graduate of the OU)

During the 1980s and 1990s I was an associate lecturer at the Open University on the third-level philosophy of the arts course, more popularly known by the OU community as AA301. The teaching was immensely challenging but tremendously enjoyable. My students were always dedicated, critical, and extremely able. They came from every walk of life and were proud to be part of the vast community that is the Open University. The OU has a small army of specialist part-time lecturers who mark a mountain of monthly essays, lead Saturday tutorials, and teach on annual summer schools. To the great relief of both tutors and students, much of the marking today is done electronically rather than through the handwritten feedback students had to decipher in the early days. The OU has been a pioneer in educational technology. Of course, introducing new technology is not unique to the Open University, but distance learning does fit neatly into the world of intranets, electronic marking, and CD-Roms. This high-tech world can be rather impersonal, but it would be wrong to think that the internet has depersonalized teaching and learning at the OU. Anyone who has attended a week-long OU summer school will testify to the heady intellectual atmosphere, the level of student support, and the sheer excitement of those five days that no amount of high-tech kit could ever match.

Figure 14: Open University students deeply engaged in intellectual discussion, a familiar sight for all those involved in adult learning.

In a few decades the university has grown from the germ of an idea to one of the world's most innovative institutions of higher education. A typical student will take six years to complete a first degree, often while working full-time, caring for a young family, or supporting an ailing or elderly relative. The OU has an impressive record of accommodating students with learning and reading disabilities and offers a sensitive and wide-ranging student support service. The thousands of students who register for the OU each new semester are a perfect illustration of the tremendous thirst for knowledge and improvement that drives so many adult students. In a relatively short space of time the OU has become successful beyond the high expectations of its founders and is now a vital part of the British cultural landscape.

The origins of the Open University can be traced back to the mid-1920s. In 1926, while working for the BBC, the historian J.C. Stobart wrote a speculative memo advocating a 'wireless university'. Stobart's vision lay dormant for 40 years before the idea resurfaced. Its time had come. The educational visionary Professor Michael Young first proposed an 'Open University' to prepare people for the external degrees of London University; Young's influence was crucial. In the 1960s both the Labour government and the BBC were considering the idea of a 'College of the Air' and in 1963 a Labour Party committee presented a report condemning the exclusion from higher education of working-class people. The report proposed a 'University of the Air', much like that proposed by Stobart and Michael Young, specifically to meet the needs of under-represented groups. These ideas were commendable and far-sighted, but required detailed thinking to convince policymakers that all this was no more than egalitarian wishful thinking or educational smoke and mirrors. Come the hour come the woman.

In 1964, Labour Prime Minister Harold Wilson made one of the most inspired appointments of his premiership when he made the indefatigable Jennie Lee Minister for the Arts. One of the first tasks Wilson set Lee was to drive forward the 'University of the Air' proposal. Wilson was obviously committed to the idea:

> Easter Sunday (1963) I spent in the Isles of Scilly. Between church and lunch I wrote the whole outline for a University of the Air.
>
> > (Harold Wilson; www.open.ac.uk,
> > accessed 23 October 2013)

Despite Wilson's enthusiasm, it is unlikely the project would have succeeded without Jennie Lee. As the OU website points out:

> Her total commitment and tenacity gradually wore down the mountains of hostility and indifference that she faced.
>
> > (www.open.ac.uk, accessed 21 September 2013)

Jennie Lee was a formidable figure and fighter for social justice. A coal miner's daughter, she was steeped in socialist politics. Her grandfather was a founder member of the Independent Labour Party and fought courageously in defence of miners and shipbuilders in Scotland's industrial heartland. Like many Scots on the political left, Jennie Lee was a prodigious reader and hard-working scholar. Her energy was legendary; she obtained a teaching diploma, a Law degree and an MA at Edinburgh University while continuing her busy political life. Citing Hardy's *Jude the Obscure* as one of her greatest influences, Lee was a great champion of adult education, supporting her husband through his two-year course at the London Labour College. An MP in Attlee's pioneering Labour Government of 1945, Lee had to wait until 1964 before she found the cause that would shape her political future.

Wilson's new Arts Minister understood the world of adult education and strongly believed this worthy but rather quirky part of the British education system should be brought into the modern world. Lee described existing adult education as she knew it at the time as, 'dowdy and mouldy ... old fashioned night schools ... hard benches'.

She might have added cold and draughty. Adult tutors such as Fred Inglis, Raymond Williams, and Richard Hoggart would recognize Lee's description of their teaching environment back in the 1950s and 1960s. Her critical comments would have sent a strong message to adult centres such as Mary Ward, Ruskin College, and the Working Men's College, all founded in the nineteenth century with a very different provenance from the budding Open University. Notwithstanding the extraordinary contribution these adult colleges made to their local communities, Lee wanted something bigger, better, and more contemporary. She took Wilson's idea for a 'University of the Air' and raised it to another level. The 1966 White Paper 'University of the Air' set the tone for the future of the OU:

> There can be no question of offering to students a makeshift project inferior in quality to other universities ... Its aim will be to provide, in addition to radio and television lectures, correspondence courses of a quality unsurpassed anywhere in the world. These will be reinforced by residential courses and tutorials.
>
> (www.open.ac.uk, accessed 21 September 2013)

There you have it. After years of research, background planning, and political persuasion, Lee's proudest political moment arrived at last in 1971 when the Open University finally opened its doors to the British public. It was Jennie Lee's greatest achievement in a long and distinguished political career. Her grandfather would have been a very proud man. In 1969 Professor Walter Perry was appointed the Open University's first vice-chancellor. Perry sowed the seeds of his fledgling institution in the unlikely setting of a grand house in Belgrave Square, where planning meetings were held in the run-up to the launch. Imagine the detailed planning needed to make the OU work: course design, assessment procedures, budgeting, building libraries, record-keeping, governance, management, tutor training, student support mechanisms, and much more. That all this was achieved in a relatively short space of time was a measure of the sheer determination and passion of those working under the leadership of Jennie Lee. But they got the job done and one of the most impressive political initiatives of the past 40 years was delivered on time. With around 70 dedicated staff, the Open University was later transferred to a small country estate on the edge of the newly established 'city' of Milton Keynes. As the vice-chancellor remarked, the move did not quite fit the utopian ideal of this exciting addition to the British educational landscape:

> That winter the site turned into a quagmire, with floods from the river and our building activities. One hundred pairs of slippers were bought to save the new carpets.
>
> (www.open.ac.uk, accessed 21 September 2013)

Slowly the physical presence of the OU began to take shape amid the grid pattern of the streets of the new city. A London-bound railway station was soon added, while Britain's newest university rose from the sodden Buckinghamshire countryside. A campus without students or teaching staff is a bizarre, almost Orwellian concept, but at least there was a library. Among the words spoken by Jennie Lee as she laid the foundation stone for the first OU library in Milton Keynes, was this declaration:

> Coming down here recalls for me, as it does for many of us, the mud right up to your eyebrows of those first years and I know that around here today there are pioneers, oh pioneers! There are some of you, of course, who came on later, you've had it easier. And of course my particular concern is that this university, which is already great, shall become greater still and that no one, no influence of any kind shall be allowed to reduce its academic status. We have established, you have established by the quality of your scholarship, you have established a university which makes *no* compromise whatsoever on academic standards, now that's its glory. But there it is a great independent university which does not insult any man or any woman whatever their background by offering them the second best, nothing but the best is good enough.
>
> (www.open.ac.uk, accessed 21 September 2013)

Despite this appeal for excellence, the years of hard work, and the OU's impressive building project, Lee's initiative had its critics. And the press reaction was hostile. The *Times Educational Supplement* of 4 March 1966 described the initiative:

> ... as vague as it is unsubstantial, just the sort of cosy scheme that shows the Socialists at their most endearing but impractical worst.

The press was lukewarm in its support, but these faint-hearted detractors, whose motivations were more ideological than educational, were soon proved wrong. Undeterred by such cynicism and supported by Arts Council chairman Lord Goodman, Secretary for Education Tony Crosland, and the BBC, Jennie Lee pressed ahead and secured the funds required to support the enterprise, not too difficult a task with the Prime Minister's backing. More serious and potentially damaging criticism came from more predictable sources. In 1969 the OU was described as 'blithering nonsense' by Tory MP Iain Macleod. Chris Christodoulou, the OU Secretary from 1969–80, recalls a visit to Milton Keynes by Macleod's colleague and future Prime Minister, Margaret Thatcher:

She came and tore us to shreds ... She even said how could we justify
spending so much money in order to satisfy the hobbies of housewives?
(www.open.ac.uk, accessed 21 September 2013)

As Richard Hoggart remarked, the birth of the OU was always going to
be a 'damn close run thing' when up against that kind of establishment
bias. As Secretary for Education, Thatcher cut OU funding by 7 per cent,
but even this spiteful measure failed to halt the university's onward march
(slowed in recent years through cuts in student funding – with predictable
results). With its famous logo, the proud new institution opened its virtual
doors to its first students in January 1971, when a staggering total of 25,000
adults registered for Level 1 programmes. They could choose from four
multidisciplinary foundation courses, in the arts, social sciences, science,
and maths. Interestingly, a large number of the first intake included teachers
wanting to convert their Certificate in Education into a full degree. Up and
running, logo chosen, funding in place, syllabus ready, and the building
programme well advanced, the questions remaining were: what were the
distinctive educational aims and objectives of this latest addition to higher
education in the UK? What did the OU actually stand for?

From the outset the OU was an educational experiment. Here
was a distance learning project on an unprecedented scale. One of its
founding premises was the conviction that communications technology
could bring higher education of the highest standard to people who, for
one reason or another, were denied the opportunity to attend traditional
campus universities. The university did not ask for entry qualifications, and
inclusivity and diversity were underlying admission principles. Students
were required to take two foundation courses before moving to the next
level, from which they could progress to a full Open University degree. This
is not unlike conventional universities where only the second and third
years count towards the final degree classification. But the OU was different
and its difference challenged conventional universities to question their own
values and methods.

First, at the new university there was a strong emphasis on teaching
study skills. A student was taught how to read academically, how to take
notes, how to develop an argument, and how to write an essay. Secondly,
assessment was progressive, with marks awarded fairly generously in the
first year, but gaining in severity over the duration of a student's degree.
Tutors' written feedback was extremely detailed and, whenever possible,
encouraging – this was the whole point of distance teaching. Thirdly, student

support was available from the very start to cater for weaker students, those with learning disabilities, or financial hardship cases.

Lastly, the majority of the early courses were multidisciplinary in nature. This commitment to subject crossover stemmed from a philosophical conviction that true knowledge cannot be split into arbitrary divisions; real depth of understanding comes from study over a broad epistemological spectrum. This multi-enquiry pedagogy aims to make connections that resemble more closely the way adults learn. This is an argument prefigured by Raphael Samuel at Ruskin College and others who have followed Samuel's example, including schools that introduced project-based learning. There are not sufficient pages here to include a full discussion on the merits of the relation between epistemology and education. Readers might refer to the debate on the subject initiated by Paul Hirst and Richard Peters (Hirst and Peters, 1970) at the London Institute of Education in the early 1970s, which had such a decisive influence on teacher training in the capital and elsewhere.

Back at the OU, where a concern with delivery began to override philosophical imperatives, teaching was delivered only at a distance. Monthly tutorials were the place for more face-to-face contact and for clarifying and developing issues that arose in that month's tutor-marked assignment (TMA), later to be renamed electronically marked assignments (EMA) as students became more computer literate. Compulsory summer schools, held a few weeks before course examinations, were the place to pull all the pieces of a course together. Most tutors and students agree that OU summer schools are among the most stimulating and effective educational environments they have experienced. Student feedback on their time at summer school confirms this admittedly anecdotal view.

Respected academics such as Arthur Marwick, Professor of History at the OU, attacked less adventurous colleagues at campus universities who argued it was simply impossible to teach degree-level courses at a distance to adults with few qualifications. What convinced Marwick and the early tutor teams they could succeed was the close partnership the OU enjoyed with the BBC. Home experiment kits for science subjects and late-night TV broadcasts have become part of the OU folklore and we all recognize the stereotypes. Technological advance has allowed the partnership to progress to the point where the BBC no longer simply broadcasts the OU courses – this can all be done online. This innovative joint venture has developed into a successful research enterprise for the benefit of a much wider public.

By the end of the 1970s, student numbers at the OU reached a staggering 70,000 with around 6,000 adults graduating each year. The university has continued to set records both in the numbers of people applying and in those achieving their degree. Sir John Horlock, OU vice-chancellor from 1981 to 1990, explained the continued success of the university in the face of political and academic opposition:

> Our main strength was in our students, both in numbers and in spirit. I had not anticipated the political pressures ... it was hardly surprising that the foundation of a university with great pride by Harold Wilson should not awaken similar feelings in a Tory government ... We had to mount a 'Save the OU' campaign. Not the least effective were the thousands of letters to MPs.
>
> (www.open.ac.uk, accessed 21 September 2013)

The OU's expansion continued throughout the 1980s and 1990s. More courses and subject areas were introduced, and the university began to offer professional training programmes alongside the more standard academic courses. In 1983 the OU opened its own Business School, which quickly gained an international reputation and is now the largest business school in Europe. In 2013, 30,000 students signed up for validated overseas programmes.

With 6,400 tutors, 1,100 full-time academic staff, and 3,500 support staff the OU can rival most building-based institutions. The OU's MA and PhD programme has an international reputation and it is now possible to study for an OU course almost anywhere in the world. Stories of students completing essays in the deserts of Africa, in the Australian bush, and on Arctic explorations are legion in the OU community – sending a buff A4 envelope to Milton Keynes containing a meticulously researched TMA from a Spanish beach or Greek island is more or less routine, although the laptop has now eliminated the need to rely on erratic local postal services.

The university's advance has been unstoppable. A pioneer in harnessing the potential of new technology for teaching and learning, from the mid-1990s the OU began to exploit the internet to the extent that it can reasonably claim to be the world's leading e-university. Brenda Gourley, vice-chancellor 2002–9, justifies the use of the internet thus:

> The future of open and distance learning lies with technology – a technology that combines with human ingenuity to deliver even more possibilities.
>
> (www.open.ac.uk, accessed 21 September 2013)

This space-age learning could not be further from classes taught in cold and remote buildings, as remembered by Jennie Lee. Ironically, this kind of fresh thinking, necessary to the university's future, also appeals to those who stood in its way back in the early 1970s. In times of austerity all education comes with a price tag, although for the political Right, cost is often a convenient excuse to turn back the educational clock. Today vocational and technical education attracts funding at the expense of courses offering intellectual purity or designed to encourage students to question and challenge prevailing orthodoxies. This point was made by Richard Hoggart back in 1995 when he wrote:

> Given these Tory governments' obsession with vocationalism and certification combined with their fear that free intellectual enquiry foments revolutionary feelings, the old style of adult education has suffered badly.
>
> (Hoggart, 1995: 52)

Hoggart is referring to the White Paper 'Education and training for the 21st century' (1992) and its distinction between 'leisure' and 'vocational training'. Funding was available for the latter, leading to a dash for cash from some rather dubious private training providers, but if you wanted to study something interesting or stimulating you paid your own way. This effectively killed off old-style adult education as we came to know it. But, as Hoggart argued, the new vocationalism was also aimed at the heart of higher education, which included the OU:

> The Open University sits, somewhat uneasily, in between these attitudes. When it was proposed, under a Labour government, its central impulse was Tawneyesque. A Tory government almost killed it at the mouth of the womb ... The compromise reached is typical: you do more clearly vocational work and we will not lean on you so heavily.
>
> (ibid.: 52)

Strong words from the author of *Uses of Literacy*, and he doesn't stop there:

> So down the drain went classes in philosophy, the plays of Shakespeare and, of course, democratic politics, as subjects of study – and everything else between these and the obviously marketable.

Adult learning, like everything else, was squeezed painfully into the values of the market. Successive vice-chancellors at the OU have dealt with these external pressures with great ingenuity. From virtual microscopes to online tutorials, the students' experience is enriched by e-media's ability to bring students closer together with their peers, tutors, and the university itself. This brave new technological world is a very long way from the late-night tutorials and handwritten essays of the early days. The OU now has the most extraordinary reach. With a special appeal to younger adults, it is the first UK university to publish materials on iTunes, where they are freely available to download. The innovative OpenLearn site and entry-level Openings courses have attracted more than one million visitors. The university's partnership with the BBC has not only been a wonderful marketing tool but has made a significant contribution to programme development. None of this could have been imagined by the OU's first VC, Walter Perry, when he said rather graphically:

> Adult education is a patch on the backside of our education system.
>
> (www.open.ac.uk, accessed 21 September 2013)

Over the past 40 years, Perry's OU, with its remarkable range of courses and high-tech delivery, has helped to dispel the dull but worthy image of adult learning. But it would be complacent to believe there are only possibilities and not threats to adults studying at the OU. Higher education funding has felt the force of the market and the 2008 economic depression. The OU and Birkbeck College have been at the forefront in persuading governments to make student funding available to all adult students, whatever their subject and however they choose to study. Despite the range of financial support available for part-time students, the costs of studying for the majority of adults at these two specialist institutions remains expensive and potentially prohibitive. Affordability has the potential to derail the OU's original mission of open access, as pressure from financial and ideological forces begins to tighten.

The Open University brought fresh thinking and new ideas to higher education in the UK. It also had little political baggage or legacy, as, for example, Ruskin College had with its historical commitment to the trade union movement and socialist ideals. Jennie Lee's original vision was taken forward by the OU in a time when old political certainties were weakening. Multiculturalism, diversity, gender, and single-issues politics defined the political and cultural landscape of the 1990s and 2000s; the old class and trade union allegiances no longer appeared relevant to a new generation of students, while older students were generally studying for personal fulfilment rather than for any political motive. The Open University was never intended to be a blue-collar institution in the manner of Ruskin and the Working Men's College, but instead became a pioneer in promoting new technology, equal opportunities, and accessibility. In that sense it has succeeded admirably, despite the severity of the opposition.

There is no typical OU student. Adults of all ages and social and cultural backgrounds choose the OU over traditional universities. They join to update their vocational skills, keep mentally active, follow a passion, or simply to prove to themselves that they can do it. A few facts and figures: 73 per cent of OU students are working, the average age of undergraduates is 29, and only 9 per cent of students are over 50. It is clearly a myth that the OU is mostly for older people: 30 per cent of new undergraduates are under 25.

The OU has a distinguished record in providing accessible programme for people with disabilities. Back in the 1990s I gave regular one-to-one philosophy tutorials to a 73-year-old student suffering from muscular dystrophy. These Saturday mornings at his house were both a delight and a privilege. He was an extremely bright student and gained a 1st-class degree, not as a result of my teaching but because he was an exceptional student who flourished within the OU's exceptional student support system.

In early 2013 the OU's student union, OUSA, agreed to place a notice in its online newsletter requesting students to make contact if they were interested in being involved in the research for this book. Within a few hours of the newsletter's publication I received a stream of emails from students willing to tell their story. After a few months I had received 78 completed response forms, with 51 stories ranging in length from 500 to 3,000 words, 33 from women and 18 from men. The age range was broad with no group dominant. Participants came from across the UK: from the remote Highlands of Scotland and from bleak housing estates in the inner cities. Most of the contributors were in the final stages of their degrees, although some had completed and moved on to postgraduate study. A few had degrees from their younger days, while others embarked on their OU course without any previous qualifications. For a significant number of the participants school had been a negative, often chilling experience. All the stories are ones of courage, personal sacrifice, and incredible resolve. Participants expressed their delight at having finally achieved the academic success that, for one reason or another, had been denied them earlier in life. A few stressed that degree-level study had transformed their previously chaotic lives and increased their confidence and self-awareness.

The participants' degree subjects ranged from English literature through to music and the sciences. They volunteered their stories and wrote with a real spirit of generosity, keen for others to learn of their experience as mature students. As such, they provide an authentic voice by which to appraise the motives, experience, and intellectual development of OU students. Distance learning students work in relative isolation, without the close camaraderie that adults at HMC and Birkbeck College enjoy, and as such are subject to different kinds of pressure. All these various factors make it difficult to build a full picture of what it is to be an OU student. But the narratives do help us to assess their motivations and the varieties of experience. If we begin by looking at the educational history of the participants, their social background, and the challenges they face, we should be able to identify any trends or patterns that emerge from the research.

OU student Louise Clark was the first person in her family to study for a degree. From a working-class background, Louise currently works as a producer at the BBC and is the only member of her team without a degree. Her OU experience has helped Louise gain the respect of her colleagues and the confidence to make her own programmes. Raising children while working in a challenging environment are routine for many women today, but few manage this while also studying part time for a degree, coping with a divorce, negotiating new relationships, and at one stage facing death threats. Louise is clearly a very exceptional person. Driven by her determination to make up for a demoralizing school experience, she seized the opportunity the OU afforded her to fulfil her considerable potential. She says she will miss studying so much when she completes her degree that she is considering registering for an MA in 2014.

Claire Baker missed most of her secondary schooling, but like many of our OU participants, she returned to learning with a vengeance. Unable to leave her house for five years due to post-traumatic stress disorder, Claire, with the aid of a tutor, gained nine GCSEs in a single academic year, including five A grades – an astonishing achievement by any standards. Armed with her newly acquired academic qualifications, Claire enrolled with the OU and is now the proud possessor of a 2.1 in science. Not content with a good undergraduate degree she has recently registered for an OU Masters in medicine. Claire wrote:

> The OU has been such a lifeline for me and now I have secured a job as a research scientist working in diagnostics. I have my life back, which is something I never thought would happen. I feel incredibly lucky that I have a passion for science that the OU helped to cultivate.

The Open University helped Louise and Claire to overcome difficult school experiences and develop belief in their own ability, while gaining qualifications to help them advance their careers. Their motives in returning to academic life were based on a desire to demonstrate they could study at this level. The progress they have made as individuals, intellectually, personally and professionally, is impressive and it is adult education that has enabled them to dramatically transform their lives.

As a youngster, Bill Brown attended a tough secondary modern school. This is his extraordinary OU story:

A JOURNEY OF ENLIGHTENMENT

I failed my 11+ (only one boy from our class of 30 passed). I can now place this failure within the context of my childhood. My parents, particularly my father, took little interest in my education. My parents were entrepreneurial business owners all through my childhood, and always too busy working to spend time overseeing my learning.

I really only enjoyed school for the last few years, before I left in 1964 with three O levels. The problem then being that in the 1960s when you left a secondary modern school, you were really only regarded as factory-fodder. This was especially the case in the south Midlands where I was living at the time. I entered into the family business with my father. All went well until the 1990s recession: I lost my father and the bank pulled the plug on my business. To help keep me sane during a period of angst and stress, I embarked on my second educational journey: with the OU Business School. This is a continuing and fascinating journey of personal development and enlightenment. I was even a guest, in my status as a successful student, at a House of Lords dinner. I graduated with my MBA in 2000. I had also built up my business again, whilst studying with the OUBS.

On reaching my early 60s, I successfully sold my business and embarked on a new chapter. I became an OUBS tutor. I teach on B122 and B120 OUBS modules and really enjoy teaching with a passion. My 50 years' practical business experience helps. I feel I have been able to help and inspire many people, as well as developing myself and my writing skills during this latest chapter.

My own education is still continuing. I have been studying for the past 18 months for an MA in education. At this stage of my journey, I hope soon to be awarded a fellowship of the Higher Education Academy along with gaining my postgraduate certificate of academic practice. Among my numerous interests is family history, and in a fuller account of my journey I would like to write about the recent discoveries I have made. Members of my family being prominent engineers, teachers, and medical professionals, early nineteenth-century university graduates, Clydeside shipbuilding owners, governors of Glasgow School of Art, an OBE ... I could go on!

Few students reach such dizzy heights as Bill. There was no privileged educational background and little parental encouragement. What he achieved, Bill did through his own efforts and the inspiration he found in the OU. Distance learning worked for Bill and it is doubtful if he could have achieved his MBA through a traditional university. Bill Brown was determined to change his life, but could not have imagined that the change would be quite so dramatic. Another OU participant who, like Bill, attended a tough secondary school was Simon Binns. Simon wrote:

> ## FROM ROUGH SLEEPER TO OU SCHOLAR
> I was kicked out of secondary school at 16, three months before my GCSEs, due to behavioural issues that related to a troubled home situation. My school allowed me in to take my exams but as I had been kicked out of home and was either sleeping rough or living in homeless shelters/hostels, I was unable to complete the exams to a good standard, although I did achieve five C-grade passes. I spent three years homeless and at the end of this time managed to get a job as a runner at an insight consultancy that based most of the methodologies around social science, mainly social anthropology. I worked my way up to a junior consultancy position in the company. Throughout my four years there I grew an interest in a need for higher education, partly as a means to accrue new knowledge but also because I was working with many people who had Masters degrees and doctorates from places like Oxford, Cambridge, and the LSE and I felt a little out of my depth (perhaps I had a slight chip on my shoulder). Later I decided to change my career, based on the experience I gained from four years with the company. I am currently studying for a BSc in Psychology with an aim to continue my studies and get an MA in Youth Psychology, and maybe one day a PhD with the OU.

Simon is in the early stage of his personal transformation from a homeless teenager to youth psychologist. He chose the OU because it allowed him to work while studying part time. Simon's motives to study at this level derive from a frustration with his school experience and a strong desire to fulfil his potential. He is well on the way to achieving his goals.

Alex Farr has been studying with the Open University for nearly two years. He is planning to complete his BA in Leadership and Management in 2014. Following his A levels, Alex worked for as a restaurant manager for KFC for a few years before his life began to unravel. Bankruptcy, depression, and problems with alcohol sent Alex into a downward spiral. One day he decided to apply for an Open University course and, slowly, he began to turn his life around. Alex believes that:

> Working on the Open University courses has given me something
> to focus on, structure, and a sense of achievement and has played
> a huge part in turning my life around. After I graduate I hope it
> will help to improve my work prospects.

One category of OU students often overlooked are people who moved to the UK from overseas. Lucia Gomez-Santana began studying psychology at the OU in 2012. She had a difficult childhood. Her mother was married at 17 and eventually had eight children. Her father died when Lucia was 6 years old, and the opportunity for a good education died with him. But thanks to the support of her brothers and sisters, as the years passed Lucia was able to study her beloved singing while studying for a Diploma in Montessori education.

She came to London with a scholarship to study voice at the Guildhall School of Music and Drama, and spent some years singing professionally. She returned to Montessori teaching while raising her two daughters and now runs her own small business, a Montessori preschool. Lucia developed an interest in psychology after learning that her mother was abused as a child.

Two years ago, one of her brothers was suddenly taken seriously ill with a brain haemorrhage. By the time Lucia arrived in Mexico her brother had lapsed into a coma. At the time she was studying with the OU and took her work with her, completing her latest assignment in Mexico. Lucia's brother passed away that year and she returned to London feeling angry and frightened, and lost interest in her studies. But encouraged by her family, she overcame her grief to complete her module, achieving a distinction in the process. Lucia then began a social psychology module, with the usual mix of excitement and trepidation. She went on to complete a child development module, applying her experience with children in an academic context. Studying with the OU helped Lucia to improve her reading, note-taking, and writing skills, which she found useful in the preparation of reports, assessments, and interviews with parents. She remembered her mother's words that 'education should not be a privilege but a right'. Lucia feels privileged to be able to pursue her passion for psychology and is keen to develop her career in that direction. Distance learning has enabled her to pursue her studies while continuing to advance her career.

Distance learning higher education has enabled thousands of people from a huge variety of backgrounds and with different motives to change their lives in the manner of Louise, Claire, Bill, Simon, Alex, and Lucia. But not all are from deprived backgrounds or experienced a poor school education. Studying for an OU degree helped Sally Black recover from a dreadful accident that left her with brain damage. Claire Baker was abused as a child and found an OU degree helped her to cope with the trauma of her childhood. Dinner lady Julie Cobbin achieved her ambition when she graduated from the OU with an honours degree. Some younger students use the OU to improve their vocational qualifications and prospects, particularly in the area of health and social care. But there are a significant number of OU students whose motivation to study is driven by their passion for an author, a period in history, a love of music, or a particular artist. In this category we have a paramedic turned specialist in English literature, a musician who turned herself into a practising scientist, and an engineer whose enthusiasm for art history developed into a Master's degree.

One such student is Dr Catherine Lee. This is her story:

THE ROAD TO A PhD

I could never have imagined, having discovered a Victorian family Bible 20 years ago, that I would take the first steps on the long road towards a PhD, a published book, and a new career as a lecturer in higher education. That Bible, found among my then recently deceased father-in-law's possessions, ignited an enthusiasm for uncovering and recording the experiences of ordinary people in the past that has stayed with me.

Other intriguing finds followed the Bible: an original 1863 marriage certificate, photographs, and another list of the names and birth dates of the same late-Victorian family. I was well and truly hooked. I threw myself into researching the history of this branch of the family. At that point, I saw an advertisement for an Open University course called 'Studying Family and Community History'. I already had a BA in Humanities, so I applied.

And so, as the saying goes, began the rest of my life. During my course I was introduced to local archives and to basic historical research skills. More compellingly, I was offered the opportunity to uncover many more individual stories and those of diverse communities, from German clerks in late-Victorian south London to Evangelical temperance workers in nineteenth-century north Kent. I learned about Charles Booth's investigations into poverty in the East End and about late eighteenth-century women preachers.

Three years later I found myself enrolling for an MA in history at the OU. I had teenage children and a part-time job. But I took the plunge. In those days of hard-copy assignments by post, life fell into a regular rhythm of racing to the post office ahead of deadline day, followed by a long agonizing wait for the postman to deliver my marked assignment. Those envelopes were ripped open with a lack of finesse that would do the average 8-year-old proud. A pleasing result would keep me elated for days and provide the motivation for the next one. There were ups and downs along the way. On the way to my first end-of-year exam I got caught up in traffic and arrived in a state of panic. A very kindly invigilator not only let me into the exam room 20 minutes late, but also allowed me extra time.

Around that time I was introduced to the topic that would eventually become the subject of my OU PhD thesis and published book. I was drawn to the Victorian preoccupation with what was euphemistically known as the 'Social Evil'. I discovered that my town was one of only 18 in the UK to be brought under legislation in the 1860s to control venereal disease by regulating prostitution. The public outcry was a significant milestone in women's history. Intriguingly, there was almost no mention of this in the local archives. I had my project topic! I discovered stories of resilience and tenacity that, I believed, deserved to be told. What really inspired me was walking on the same streets and past the same buildings as the people who appeared in the documents and old newspapers.

I enjoyed writing up the dissertation and was delighted on Christmas Eve 2003 when my results letter arrived with the Christmas post, informing me that I had gained the degree of Master of Arts in History with distinction. I got the predictable lump in the throat at the graduation ceremony when I received my degree from Baroness Boothroyd. That was such a great thrill. Before too long, however, the itch returned. I believed at the time that my topic could be developed into a PhD thesis. I applied and the interview went well. I met my prospective supervisors and was soon looking at the prospect of another six years studying with the OU. I started to feel that I really belonged in the OU, so when a full-time studentship became available within the Arts faculty I applied. After a long and intense selection day, I was delighted to be told I got the job.

With enormous encouragement I was able to deliver my thesis on time. I hoped that the end product stayed true to the spirit of that initial ambition to uncover the untold stories of ordinary women who eked out an existence in the dockyard and port towns of Kent in the second half of the nineteenth century. I survived the viva and emerged from the examination room a Doctor of Philosophy, exactly ten years after completing that very first module.

What next? By chance, the OU was preparing to launch its brand-new Arts foundation module, 'The Arts: Past and Present'. With one term's experience teaching undergraduates at a local university as my credentials, I applied and was fortunate to be appointed. I now tutor across the OU first-year Arts modules. As a former OU student I am able to empathize with new undergraduates. In December 2012 my first book, based on my OU PhD thesis, was published. And, yes, I'm still studying. I have now embarked on an OU Master of Education degree, to help me become a better teacher.

Caroline's story is not just about social justice, building communities, or the class struggle. It is about one woman's efforts to realize her academic potential and follow her intellectual curiosity through distance learning. Caroline paid her own course fees, as many OU students do. Her story is an illustration of what can be achieved in what Raymond Williams described as 'a fully participatory and educated democracy'. The Open University is a living embodiment of the social and political philosophy that can no longer be described as socialism, but that nonetheless centres on the principles of human generosity, civility, and opportunity. The OU is accessible whether you have a disability, are a recovering addict, homeless, or wishing to improve your career prospects. Many students are desperately trying to make up for inadequate schooling, or live in a remote part of Britain, like Rose Papai. Living in the Scottish Highlands was no obstacle for Rose. Her studies with the OU helped her to progress from classroom assistant to headteacher in just a few years.

There are hundreds of OU stories like the ones above, tales of people who have transformed their lives through distance learning. Those included are a representative sample of the different categories of people who make up the university's student body. The OU may not reach deep into the deprived inner cities in the manner of centres such as Mary Ward and the Working Men's College, nor have the political concerns of Ruskin College. But in its way, the OU is one distinctive thread that contributes to the rich texture of adult learning in the UK; indeed, it is one of its most vivid colours. The success of the Open University is a ringing endorsement of the educational vision of Michael Young and Harold Wilson and the tenacity of Jennie Lee. The skilful leadership of those early vice-chancellors, Walter Perry, Sir John Horlock, and Brenda Gourley, has ensured that each year thousands of adult students continue to enjoy the opportunity to study within the virtual walls of this very special institution, often at great financial sacrifice.

Endnote

Writing in August 2014, I detect some signs that the adult education sector is beginning to stage a fight-back against government expenditure cuts. We know from the history of adult learning that the sector has been defended by historians and cultural theorists such as Raymond Williams, Carolyn Steedman, Paulo Freire, and Edward Thompson. Their defence took the form of constructing and promoting a theoretical framework within which the sector functioned effectively for 40 years. Over a century earlier, Mary Ward, George Birkbeck, and two young Americans in Oxford and the founders of the Working Men's College in London worked boldly and with great imagination to provide a structural and educational foundation for the sector, which survives to this day.

This book shows how adult learning was initially aimed at improving the literacy and numeracy of skilled working men. There have been three major developments in the sector since the establishment of the WMC in 1854. First, from the late 1970s the majority of adult students have been women. Secondly, in the twentieth century the urban middle class replaced 'blue collar' workers as the main beneficiaries of adult education. Thirdly, in our major towns and cities the sector has succeeded in meeting the educational needs of a multi-ethnic and multilingual population – a later development that can be viewed as a correction to the appropriation of adult education by an emergent bourgeoisie.

The aims and objectives of adult learning have shifted from a concern with class struggle and feminism to much more general and encompassing notions of respect, social justice, community capacity building, and a more generalized equality. We have seen how, building on the principles of the founders, inner-city adult centres such as the Mary Ward Centre, Birkbeck College, and the WMC have worked tirelessly to become more accessible and welcoming to immigrant communities and minorities in general. Outreach programmes, English-language classes, and community learning have become a priority, as have retention and progression. Within these developments, tutors have modified their teaching to include a genuine respect for their students, negotiating schemes of work and curriculum, and differentiation of delivery to suit differing abilities and levels.

Of course, this is not the whole story. We have seen from the student stories in the book that people come to adult learning for any number of reasons and motivations. The sector has always been more than just about theoretical posturing or social and political intervention as many in the sector would like to think. Personal fulfilment, career motives, recovery from dependency and addiction, and health and well-being are among the myriad reasons why adults sign up for classes. These may or may not be included within ideas about social justice and capacity building. I return to Raymond Williams's contention that a healthy and seriously funded adult education sector ought to be a dynamic part of what constitutes an 'educated and participatory democracy' in which equality and social justice are essential principles. One of its great virtues is that adult learning allows people to breathe, flourish, and achieve their full potential. A healthy adult sector is a sign of a confident and civilized culture. The creativity and resolve of adult educators will ensure the sector grows and achieves its aims providing the political will is strong. We need to move away from a sector that is in continual crisis to one that is respected as an essential part of our education system.

It has been refreshing to escape the enveloping fog of theory for a time and to hear the participants talk excitedly and with real passion about their studies. So the last word must go to one of them, and I chose a student who remembers his secondary modern school experience as being one of the most damaging of his life. Recent governments have encouraged sharper divisions of inequality, put schools out to the market, and removed local accountability. Children are set according to their social class long before they reach secondary school, and with the end of the comprehensive ideal we are witnessing the return to a neo-elitist model of compulsory schooling. Those from poor homes and deprived backgrounds are held back not by poor teachers, but by poverty and disadvantage. Within this political climate promise and potential are crushed and defeated, so it is likely that adult learning will be needed as much in the future as it was back in 1854.

> I am pleased to say that I will have an MSc in Forensic Psychology & Criminology conferred on me on 31 December 2013 and that I will indeed have gained the highest academic award of my life. I feel very privileged to have had a university education and in some respects I feel that, although I did it for myself, I also did it on behalf of all the other young people who were in my class at school who I am sure had the ability to do what I did; some would have achieved much more but sadly they did not have the opportunity.

> (Allen Jack)

References

Andrews, G., Kean, H., and Thompson, J. (1999) *Ruskin College: Contesting knowledge, dissenting politics*. London: Lawrence and Wishart.

Bate, J. (2003) *John Clare: A biography*. London: Picador.

Birch, C. (2013) *Researching Learning Cultures and Educational Identities in Communities*. Leicester: NIACE.

Burns, D.C. (1924) *A Short History of Birkbeck College*. University of London Press.

Caldwell, P. (2013). Online. www.annwalkerwea.wordpress.com/ (accessed 15 March 2014).

Coe, S. (2012) *Running My Life: The autobiography*. London: Hodder and Stoughton.

Fieldhouse, R. (1996) *A History of Modern British Adult Education*. Leicester: NIACE.

Fieldhouse, R. and Associates (2001) *A History of Modern Adult Education*. Leicester: NIACE.

Freire, P. (1972) *Pedagogy of the Oppressed*. Harmondsworth: Penguin.

Gillies, M. (2011) *The Barbed-Wire University: The real lives of Allied prisoners of war in the Second World War*. London: Aurum.

Harrison, J.F.C. (1954) *A History of the Working Men's College 1854–1954*. London: Routledge and Kegan Paul.

Hirst, P.H. and Peters, R.S. (1970) *The Logic of Education*. Abingdon/New York: Routledge and Kegan Paul.

Hirst, P.H. and White, P.A. (eds) (1998) *Philosophy of Education: Major themes in the analytic tradition*. London/New York: Routledge.

Hoggart, R. (1995) *The Way We Live Now: Dilemmas in contemporary culture*. London: Chatto and Windus.

Inglis, F. (2014) *Richard Hoggart: Virtue and reward*. Cambridge: Polity Press.

Kelly, T. (1992) *A History of Adult Education in Great Britain: From the Middle Ages to the twentieth century*. Liverpool: Liverpool University Press.

Loach, K. (2013) *Spirit of '45*. Online. www.spiritof45.org (accessed 15 November 2013).

Rose, J. (2001) *Intellectual Life of the British Working Classes*. New Haven and London: Yale University Press.

Ruskin Students' Labour History Pamphlets No. 1: 'Education and the Working Class at Ruskin College 1889–1909'. Oxford.

Simon, B. (ed.) (1990) *The Search for Enlightenment: The working class and adult education in the 20th century*. London: Lawrence and Wishart.

Steedman, C. (1989) 'Writing, Teaching and Learning'. Unpublished conference paper, University of Warwick.

Sutherland, J. (1991) *Mrs Humphry Ward: Eminent Victorian, pre-eminent Edwardian*. Oxford: Oxford University Press.

Taylor, P. (1993) *The Texts of Paulo Freire*. Buckingham: Open University Press.

Philip Stevens

Thompson, E.P. (1968) *The Making of the English Working Class.*
London: Pelican.
Williams, R. (1999) *An Open Letter to WEA Tutors.* London: Workers'
Educational Association.

Further reading

Freire, P. (1995) *Pedagogy of Hope: Reliving pedagogy of the oppressed.* New
York: Continuum.
Harris, K. (1979) *Education and Knowledge.* London: Routledge and Kegan Paul.
Hirst, P.H. and White, P.A. (eds) (1998) *Philosophy of Education: Major themes in
the analytic tradition.* London: Routledge.
Hoggart, R. (1957) *The Uses of Literacy: Aspects of working class life.*
London: Penguin.
Morgan, W.J. and Preston, P. (1993) *Raymond Williams: Politics, education, letters.*
New York: St Martin's Press.
Pollins, H. (1984) *The History of Ruskin College.* Oxford: Ruskin College Library.
Williams, R. (1984) *The Long Revolution.* Harmondsworth: Pelican.

Index